EU CLIMATE POLICY EXPLAINED

The EU is the region of the world where the most climate policies have been implemented, and where practical policy experimentation in the field of the environment and climate change has been taking place at a rapid pace over the last twenty-five years. This has led to considerable success in reducing pollution, decoupling emissions from economic growth and fostering global technological leadership.

The objective of the book is to explain the EU's climate policies in an accessible way, and to demonstrate not only the step-by-step approach that has been used to develop these policies, but also the ways in which they have been tested and further improved in the light of experience. The book shows that there is no single policy instrument that can reduce greenhouse gas emissions, but the challenge has been to put a jigsaw of policy instruments together that is coherent, delivers emission reductions, and is cost-effective. The book differs from existing books in that it covers the EU's emissions trading system, the energy sector and other economic sectors, including their development in the context of international climate policy.

Set against the backdrop of the 2015 UN Climate Change Conference in Paris, this accessible book will be of great relevance to students, scholars and policymakers alike.

Jos Delbeke has been the Director-General of the European Commission's Directorate-General for Climate Action since its creation in 2010 (ongoing). He holds a Ph.D. in economics (Louvain, 1986) and lectures at the University of Louvain, Belgium, on European and international environmental policy.

Peter Vis is the EU Visiting Fellow at St. Antony's College, University of Oxford, UK, for the academic year 2014–15. Prior to that he was Head of Cabinet to Connie Hedegaard, European Commissioner for Climate Action (2010–14). He has an MA (history) from the University of Cambridge, UK.

EU CLIMATE POLICY EXPLAINED

Edited by
Jos Delbeke and
Peter Vis

WITH GER KLAASSEN, JÜRGEN LEFEVERE, DAMIEN MEADOWS,
ARTUR RUNGE-METZGER, YVON SLINGENBERG,
STEFAAN VERGOTE, JAKE WERKSMAN AND PETER ZAPFEL

LONDON AND NEW YORK

First published 2015
by Routledge
2 Park Square, Milton Park, Abingdon, Oxon OX14 4RN

and by Routledge
711 Third Avenue, New York, NY 10017

Routledge is an imprint of the Taylor & Francis Group, an informa business

© 2015 European Union

The information and views set out in this book are those of the authors and do not necessarily reflect those of the European Commission.

British Library Cataloguing-in-Publication Data
A catalogue record for this book is available from the British Library.

Library of Congress Cataloging in Publication Data
A catalogue record for this book has been requested.

ISBN: 978-92-79-48263-2 (hbk)
ISBN: 978-92-79-48261-8 (pbk)
ISBN: 978-92-79-48260-1 (ebk)

Typeset in Bembo
by Apex CoVantage, LLC

CONTENTS

FIGURES AND TABLES

Figures

Tables

FOREWORD

The development and implementation of climate policies, and their adjustment over time, must be informed by experience and lessons learned. This book appraises the EU's climate policy instruments, how initial choices of instrument have been adjusted, how effective they have been, and where we are going in terms of adapting these instruments to the challenges ahead. It also gives an overview of the international negotiations on climate change.

The authors are those who have been working on these policies in the European Commission, and who possess the insights acquired and now shared.

Policymaking is not about what can be done in theory, but much inspired by practicalities and political feasibility. This is also the case for climate policy in the specific context of the European Union. Starting points for policies are not always ideal or fully in line with economic or legal theory, but where else to start from, if not from how things are? Some would like the international climate negotiations, or the actions of third countries, to be very different from what they are. Such wishful thinking must not detract from need for progress; we must avoid the perfect being the enemy of the good.

The science makes clear how much more needs to be done to effectively tackle dangerous climate change from impacting on the planet and its people. The effectiveness and costs of policies will be key to determining the pace of progress. The EU is making its share of efforts needed to reduce greenhouse gas emissions and has put in place ambitious climate policies leading to a true decoupling of emissions and economic growth. But the problem of climate change is obviously not one that the EU can solve alone. Fortunately, the experience of the EU, can also serve as valuable learning-by-doing for other countries, as they develop their climate policies while putting their economies on a solid track towards prosperous, low-carbon development.

I commend the authors for their contributions to this book and for their relentless efforts for an ambitious EU climate policy throughout the years. I am confident that through developing low-carbon pathways and taking up innovative technologies and best practices, we can make our common objective of averting dangerous climate change a success – starting with a robust agreement at COP21 in Paris in December 2015!

Miguel Arias Cañete
European Commissioner for Climate Action & Energy

ACKNOWLEDGEMENTS

The authors would like to thank Jenny Avery, Hans Bergman, Ilona Billaux-Koman, Jolene Cook, Jan Cornillie, Raya Corry-Fitton, Ben Gill, Polona Gregorin, Christian Holzleitner, Alan Huyton, Anna Johansson, Arno Kaschl, Simon Kay, Edas Kazakevicius, Ariane Labat, Roel Merckx, Alexandre Paquot, Cornelius Rhein, Piotr Tulej, Tom Van Ierland and Kaveh Zahedi for comments, suggestions and support.

CONTRIBUTORS

Jos Delbeke joined the European Commission in 1986 and has been the Director-General of the Directorate-General for Climate Action since its creation in 2010. He was closely involved in negotiations on the 2020 and 2030 policy packages on climate change and energy. He holds a Ph.D. in economics (Louvain, 1986) and in 1985 worked at the International Monetary Fund (Washington, DC, USA). He lectures at the University of Leuven, Belgium, on European and international environmental policy.

Ger Klaassen is Policy Analyst on Strategy and Economic Assessment at the European Commission's Directorate-General for Climate Action. Before joining the Commission, he worked as an economist at the International Institute for Applied Systems Analysis. He holds a Ph.D. in economics from the Free University in Amsterdam, the Netherlands. He was Visiting Professor at Colorado College in Colorado Springs, USA, and the University of Economics and Business Administration in Vienna, Austria, teaching environmental economics and innovation.

Jürgen Lefevere is currently on sabbatical leave from the European Commission. Until July 2014, he was Adviser on International and Climate Strategy at the Directorate-General for Climate Action. Prior to joining the Commission in 2003, he worked at the London-based Foundation for International Environmental Law and Development. He has a law degree from the University of Maastricht and was a research associate on EU environmental policy (1993–8).

Damien Meadows is the Adviser on European and International Carbon Markets at the European Commission's Directorate-General for Climate Action. Before this he was Head of the Directorate-General's Unit for the International Carbon Market, Aviation and Maritime. He is a solicitor of the High Court of England and Wales. Before joining the European Commission in 2001, he worked for the UK government and in private practice, as well as with the United Nations Climate Change Secretariat.

Artur Runge-Metzger is the Director on International & Climate Strategy at the European Commission's Directorate-General for Climate Action. He spent two years in the EU Delegation in Sarajevo/Bosnia and Herzegovina, and worked in the Directorate-General for Development, the Directorate-General for the Environment in Brussels and the EU Delegation in Harare/Zimbabwe. He holds a Ph.D. in agricultural economics from the Georg-August-University in Göttingen, Germany. From June 2013 to December 2014, he served as co-chair of the Ad Hoc Working Group on the Durban Platform for Enhanced Action preparing the new global climate agreement to be concluded in Paris in 2015.

Yvon Slingenberg is Senior Adviser in the Cabinet of Commissioner Miguel Arias Cañete. She was previously Head of the Unit for Implementation of the EU ETS in the European Commission's Directorate-General for Climate Action. She joined the Commission in 1993 and is a lawyer with a degree in international law (specialisation in environmental law) from the University of Amsterdam, the Netherlands.

Stefaan Vergote is Head of the Unit for Economic Analysis and Financial Instruments at the European Commission's Directorate-General for Energy. He was previously Head of the Unit for Strategy and Economic Analysis in the Directorate-General for Climate Action. He holds a degree in electro-mechanical engineering and a postgraduate degree in environmental management from the University of Leuven, Belgium.

Peter Vis is the EU Visiting Fellow at St. Antony's College, University of Oxford, UK, for the academic year 2014–15. He was Head of Cabinet to Connie Hedegaard, European Commissioner for Climate Action from 2010–14. Before joining the European Commission in 1990, he worked for the UK's tax and customs authority (HM Revenue & Customs). He has an MA (history) from the University of Cambridge, UK.

Jake Werksman is Principal Adviser to the European Commission's Directorate-General for Climate Action, where his work focuses on the international dimensions of European climate policy. Before joining the Commission in 2012, he held posts at the World Resources Institute, the Rockefeller Foundation, United Nations Development Programme, and the Foundation for International Environmental Law and Development in London. He has lectured in international environmental and economic law at master's level at the New York University Law School, USA; Georgetown University Law Center, USA; and at the School of Oriental and African Studies and University College at the University of London, UK. He holds degrees from Columbia University, USA (A.B.), the University of Michigan, USA (J.D.), and the University of London (LL.M.).

Peter Zapfel is Head of the Unit for Implementation of the EU ETS in the European Commission's Directorate-General for Climate Action. Prior to his current assignment he was Assistant to the Director-General, responsible for policy coordination and economic assessment. He holds academic degrees from the University of Business and Economics in Vienna, Austria, and the John F. Kennedy School of Government at Harvard University, USA.

EDITORS' INTRODUCTION

Jos Delbeke and Peter Vis

Go as far as you can see; when you get there you'll be able to see farther.
Thomas Carlyle, Scottish philosopher (1795–1881)

The purpose of this book is to explain the European Union's climate policies to the interested but not necessarily specialist reader. The main theme
is that the EU has been the place in the world where, over the last quarter
of a century, active learning has characterised policymaking in the field of
the environment and climate change. This has led to considerable success
in cleaning up pollution, decoupling emissions from economic growth and
fostering global technological leadership.

A first important lesson is that European climate policy has been built up
step by step. Learning-by-doing has turned out to be a key feature. Tackling
the new and complex problem of climate change means that many consumers and producers need to change their habits and reduce greenhouse
gas emissions. It is like changing the course of a huge supertanker at sea: it
requires time. Such changes also have many economy-wide repercussions.
This has all needed to be done in a rapidly changing world, and in a multi-
level regulatory environment, such as exists in the EU.

In the 1990s, economists were actively looking at how to improve environmental policymaking, and made a strong case for putting a price on the
impacts of pollution that are not otherwise paid for by the polluter ('pricing
environmental externalities'). Their preferred way to do this was through
taxation, and the EU tried for almost a decade to get a carbon-energy tax

adopted. This failed for political reasons, as the notion of creating new taxes was an unpopular message at a time when many people already felt over-taxed. This also failed for institutional reasons, as European taxes need to be adopted with the unanimous agreement of the Member States, which proved impossible. An alternative approach, limiting the quantity of pollution, was subsequently preferred to imposing a fixed tax on pollution.

One of the most striking examples of learning-by-doing concerns the EU's emissions trading system, where initially the allocation of allowances was made by EU Member States, predominantly on the basis of free handouts to private companies. While it was generally known that this was sub-optimal, it was a necessary step to get the system in place. Quite quickly, on the basis of the experience gained, consensus grew that better solutions were needed and allocation now takes place on the basis of auctioning and EU-wide performance benchmarks.

Similarly, the emission reduction policy for passenger cars was initially based on Voluntary Agreements with the car industry in the late 1990s. These did not work as intended and so were replaced by binding, but flexible, legislation. Learning-by-doing in policymaking is important; no new policy approach will ever be perfect from the outset, especially in a rapidly changing world.

A second important lesson is that there is no 'silver bullet', no one single policy instrument, suited to bring down greenhouse gas emissions across so many sectors of economic activities. Different approaches are called for across different economic sectors. The art is therefore in putting together a 'jigsaw' of policy approaches that is effective, coherent and cost-effective. At the same time, it is important to avoid double regulation or overlaps between different instruments, as these may give conflicting signals to economic operators.

A third lesson is that solid economic and technical preparation of policy, as well as extensive stakeholder consultation, is of the utmost importance. This is not only necessary to gain sufficient understanding and backing at political level, but also to make sure that the policy context – once agreed – remains as stable as possible. There are often high, and largely conflicting, economic interests at stake, and creating maximum transparency has been a necessary precondition for success. Our experience has shown that policymaking on the basis of facts and figures, an explicit analysis of costs and benefits to society, and an active engagement with stakeholders has been more rewarding than overly concentrating on what is considered politically opportune in the short term.

While the journey of building up a comprehensive climate policy in the EU started in the 1990s, it really took-off around the year 2000, when the Kyoto Protocol was approved but work to have it ratified was still ongoing.

Given the huge task that the decarbonisation of Europe implies, a decade and a half is a short period of time. It is too early, therefore, to make a final assessment of the EU's climate change policy experience. Nevertheless the following key elements are already emerging:

1   The EU has demonstrated that emissions can be reduced while economic growth continues: between 1990 and 2013, GDP of the 28 Member States increased by 45% while emissions were reduced by 19%. In times of recession, as might be expected, the trend of steadily falling emissions continues.

2   The EU has successfully used market mechanisms to reduce emissions, in particular by putting a price on carbon. This pricing process has worked its way through the economy in a consistent manner, as a result of which relatively easy and inexpensive reductions of emissions were achieved. However the most severe economic recession of the post-war period, starting in 2008, has caused sub-optimal market functioning that still needs to be corrected.

3   The EU has been a leader in deploying low-carbon and energy-efficient technologies, both in new sectors, such as renewable energy, as well as in more traditional industrial sectors, such as the automotive, chemicals and steel sectors. Significantly, the EU is a global leader in the number of patents registered for low-carbon technologies.

4   The integration of the climate dimension in the design of policies with economic relevance, such as energy, transport, industry, or regional development, has been crucial. This is important at all levels: EU, national and local. New initiatives taken locally are promising, such as those developed under the Covenant of the Mayors.

5   Businesses ask for a stable regulatory environment, directed at long-term structural changes rather than short-term policy interventions and regulatory changes. That is why European leaders have already decided on a climate and energy policy framework for 2030, confirming and accelerating the now established trend towards decarbonisation, and placing emphasis on a stronger carbon constraint as well as on renewable energy and highly energy-efficient equipment.

The policy landscape will continue to evolve in the light of experience and circumstances, while endeavouring to provide maximum predictability for businesses and consumers. Consolidation of some of these new policies has taken time, and a further revision of much of the legislation explained in this book is to be expected. This will happen when implementing the 2030 framework for climate and energy policy. These changes will offer another opportunity not to reinvent policy approaches, which are now established and proving their worth, but to 'fine-tune' them so as to increase their effectiveness.

We hope this book will be valuable to all those involved in policymaking, not least in countries starting to set up their own climate policies, as well as the academic reader interested in how and why policies implemented may sometimes differ from textbook theory.

This book is deliberately written with a minimum of jargon and abbreviations, a particularly challenging task in the field of climate policy. The purpose of each chapter is to explain why and how policies have been developed, and the experience with them so far. Each section ends with a brief conclusion. For those interested in the complete texts of EU legislation, ample references are made to the websites where these can be found.

This book has the following structure. Chapter 1 describes the EU's climate policy leadership in a changing world, ending with the proposed framework for a climate and energy framework for 2030. Chapter 2 describes the workings of the core piece of EU climate policy: the EU Emissions Trading System (EU ETS). Chapter 3 summarises how the EU's energy-related policies not only improve energy security but also contribute to reducing the EU's greenhouse gas emissions. Chapter 4 is of a cross-cutting nature and describes a range of EU policies that help Member States to reduce greenhouse gas emissions in the sectors not covered by the EU ETS. Chapter 5 describes the international developments from the signing of the Kyoto Protocol to the present, in the run-up to the comprehensive climate agreement that so urgently needs to be agreed in Paris in 2015. Finally, Chapter 6 makes some concluding remarks on the future outlook.

1

EU CLIMATE LEADERSHIP IN A RAPIDLY CHANGING WORLD

Jos Delbeke and Peter Vis

Compelling scientific evidence

Climate change is an environmental problem that is very different from the more traditional areas of pollution, such as water, waste or air quality. Greenhouse gas emissions do not have a direct impact on human health: they are not visible and do not smell. Moreover, climate change is a truly global environmental problem, as it does not matter at all where greenhouse gases are emitted – they have the same impact. Such greenhouse gas emissions are predominantly related to the use of fossil fuels that have been massively used since the Industrial Revolution that started in Europe in the late eighteenth century, mostly coal and later oil and gas. In the light of emerging uncertainties in the early 1980s, one of the most important decisions at the international level was to create in 1988 the Intergovernmental Panel on Climate Change (IPCC) as a forum for the world's scientists to come forward with a consensual view on what climate science can say.

The 'Summary for Policymakers' of the IPCC's Fifth Assessment Report of Working Group I, finalised in 2013, made a number of key statements in a very clear manner. The most important ones were that: 'Warming of the climate system is unequivocal, and since the 1950s, many of the observed changes are unprecedented over decades to millennia' and that 'Human influence on the climate system is clear' (IPCC, 2013: 6).

From its assessment, the IPCC also concluded that continued emissions of greenhouse gases will cause further changes to the atmosphere, land and oceans in all regions of the world, many of which would continue for centuries even if further emissions ceased. Thus, the science points to the inevitable conclusion that if we are to limit future climate change and avoid catastrophic, potentially irreversible impacts, we need to make significant and immediate reductions in global greenhouse gas emissions. As climate scientist James Hansen put it: 'Imagine a giant asteroid on a direct collision course with Earth. That is the equivalent of what we face now [with climate change], yet we dither.'[1]

The IPCC's Fifth Assessment Report is the culmination of years of effort to examine the vast body of scientific literature on climate change. The report's contribution to the physical climate science confirms and strengthens the findings of previous assessments using new evidence. It draws on more extensive observations, improved climate models, greater understanding of climate processes and feedbacks, and a wider range of climate change projections.

Assessing the literature is a significant undertaking which must examine multiple strands of evidence to produce coherent messages that accurately reflect the science. To this end, the report is subject to a robust, open and transparent review process which involves both scientific experts and governments around the world. Ultimately, though, the scientists have the final word and that final word remains firmly rooted in the scientific evidence. For the IPCC's Working Group I report, this evidence was provided in over 9,000 peer-reviewed papers published since 2007 and assessed by over 850 scientists involved as authors, contributors or review editors. A further 1,000 or so experts were also involved in the review process. On this basis, the high degree of scientific consensus becomes undeniable.

While some prominence has been given in the media to a slower increase in global surface temperature over the past 15 years (see Figure 1.1, top part panel (a)), the scientific community and policymakers remain focused on the risks posed by human-induced climate change of the more relevant long-term trend. Over short timescales, typically considered to be periods of fewer than 30 years, surface temperatures are strongly dominated by natural fluctuations in the earth's climate that mask the influence of increasing concentrations of greenhouse gases in the atmosphere. Examination of the longer-term trend, however, shows a much clearer picture of what lies ahead. The last three decades have been successively warmer than all preceding decades on record (lower part panel (a) Figure 1.1).

Figure 1.1 covers the period from 1850 to 2012 (the last year for which data were available when the IPCC report of 2013 was published). Changes are given as changes compared to the average temperature in the period

1961 to 1990. In 2012, for example, the annual average was more than 0.4°C higher than in the period 1961 to 1990 (upper panel Figure 1.1). In the last decade (2000–2010) the global temperature was around 0.45°C higher than the 1961–1990 period (lower panel Figure 1.1).

Despite some past periods where global temperature has been stable or even decreased, it is irrefutable that overall the planet is warming. Temperature changes are uneven across the globe, and regional observations show that land areas are warming more than the ocean surface, and that some regions, the Arctic and Africa for example, are warming much faster than others (see part (b) of Figure 1.1).

Change in global average surface temperature, however, is just a small part of the much bigger global warming and climate change picture. Observations of multiple indicators of climate change all reveal a consistent message that the planet is gaining energy, leading to warming of the climate system as a whole. More than 90% of the additional energy resulting from increasing greenhouse gas concentrations is stored in the world's oceans and this is having measurable and unprecedented impacts. Sea level has been observed to be rising at an increasing pace as a result of the expansion of oceans as they warm, and as a result of additional water from melting glaciers and the large ice sheets of Greenland and Antarctica. The extent of Arctic sea ice is also decreasing and it is projected that, if no efforts are made to reduce greenhouse gas emissions, the Arctic could be nearly ice free in September before the middle of the twenty-first century.

On the basis of an increasing body of evidence, the EU's Environment Council already agreed in 1996 to limit global average surface temperature rise to below 2°C (3.6°F) above pre-industrial levels[2] to prevent the most severe impacts of climate change or dangerous human interference with the climate system. In March 2007 the European Council, i.e. the EU Heads of State and Government, underlined the vital importance of achieving the strategic objective of limiting the global average temperature increase to not more than 2°C above pre-industrial levels.[3] In 2014 many world leaders also endorsed this commitment in 2014, at a Summit organised by UN Secretary-General Ban Ki-moon.[4]

To be exact, however, science does not specify a 'safe' level of temperature rise, but recognises that, as temperature increases, climate impacts worsen and the risk of triggering catastrophic and potentially irreversible changes increases. To make it likely (a probability of 66–100%) to stay within the 2°C average temperature increase, global greenhouse gas emissions (expressed in CO_2-equivalent emissions) would have to be reduced between 41% and 72% in 2050 compared to 2010. In the year 2100 global greenhouse gas

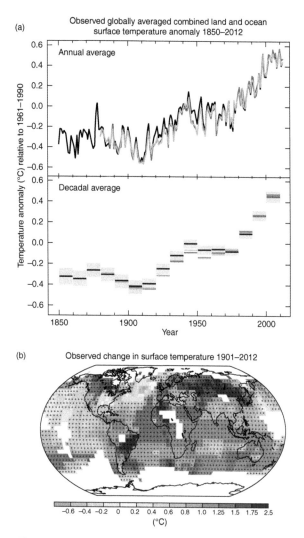

FIGURE 1.1 Figure SPM.1 (a) Observed global mean combined land and ocean surface temperature anomalies, from 1850 to 2012 from three data sets. Top panel: annual mean values. Bottom panel: decadal mean values including the estimate of uncertainty for one dataset (black). Anomalies are relative to the mean of 1961–1990. (b) Map of the observed surface temperature change from 1901–2012 derived from temperature trends determined by linear regression from one dataset (lighter-coloured line in panel (a)). Trends have been calculated where data availability permits a robust estimate (i.e. only for grid boxes with greater than 70% complete records and more than 20% data availability in the first and last 10% of the time period). Other areas are white. Grid boxes where the trend is significant at the 10% level are indicated by a + sign. For a listing of the datasets and further technical details see the Technical Summary.

Source: IPCC (2013).

reductions would have to be between 78% and 118% lower than emissions in 2010 (IPCC, 2014: 22). Reductions of more than 100% are possible if biomass is burned in power plants and the resulting CO_2 emissions are captured and stored. In this way CO_2-equivalent concentrations are kept at levels of around 450 parts per million (ppm), consistent with a likely chance of keeping global warming below 2°C over the twenty-first century relative to pre-industrial levels.

The scientific evidence suggests that, while meeting the 2°C objective is challenging, it remains possible. The basic implication is that the world must stop the growth in global greenhouse gas emissions by around 2020, and reduce emissions by at least half of 1990 levels by the middle of this century and continue cutting them thereafter. In this context the European Union has reaffirmed that developed countries as a group should continue to take the lead and should reduce their greenhouse gas emissions by 80–95% by 2050 compared to 1990.[5]

Conclusion: the planet is warming at an unprecedented speed, measured not only over decades but also over millennia. This is caused by humans and due mainly to the huge consumption of fossil fuels since the beginning of the Industrial Revolution. Scientists tell us that it is possible to contain the worst impacts of climate change, provided we keep global temperature increases below 2°C compared to pre-industrial times. For that reason EU and world leaders have confirmed the importance of the below-2°C objective.

The EU has a strong multilateral tradition

As part of the new post-war world order, the European nations strongly supported the creation of multilateral institutions, known as the 'Pax Americana'. In fact, the EU's own institutional development is an expression of that same multilateralism. Today, there is a strong belief by Europeans that global problems need to be addressed multilaterally, in the context of the United Nations (UN), despite concerns and disappointments regarding its efficiency and effectiveness.

In the field of environmental protection, the UN has been the preferred forum for discussing issues related to trans-boundary pollution. In the 1970s, questions relating to the environment were the subject of political debate in the wake of the reports of the Club of Rome (see in particular Meadows et al., 1972), to a large extent responding to the first compelling evidence of a demographic explosion. The sustainability question was elevated for the first time to the UN level in Stockholm in 1972 and taken over with vigour, among others, by Ms Gro Harlem Brundtland, the then Prime Minister of Norway and Chairperson of the World Commission on Environment and Development in its report 'Our Common Future' (1987).

This led to the 1992 'Earth Summit' in Rio de Janeiro at which was agreed the UN Framework Convention on Climate Change (UNFCCC), following convincing scientific evidence related to climate change. Five years later the Kyoto Protocol was agreed (1997) in which developed countries committed to take the lead in reducing greenhouse gas emissions by committing to quantitative emission reductions and limitation targets.

Ratification of the Kyoto Protocol by the EU and its Member States was finalised in April 2002, but by that time the US had decided not to follow up its signature by ratification. This was a major blow to the Kyoto Protocol, but it nevertheless entered into force thanks to ratification by a sufficient number of countries including, crucially, the Russian Federation. The Kyoto Protocol created the platform for the EU to start developing a comprehensive set of policies specifically targeted to reduce greenhouse gas emissions. These policies largely contributed to the EU overachieving its target of 8% reduction compared to 1990 by the end of the Protocol's first commitment period in 2012.

Climate change, together with ozone depletion, represents a new generation of environmental issues that are truly global in nature. Irrespective of where the emissions of ozone-depleting substances or of carbon dioxide occur in the world, their impact is global. That is why there is such a need for global action. For the EU, the UN is the obvious level at which to act, as is widely recognised by public opinion.

Since 1992, however, the world has changed a great deal. Back then, the world was divided between developed and developing nations. Today, more than 20 years later, the EU, the US and Japan represent a lower share of world economic activity, due to the impressive emergence of new industrial players, not least in Asia. This also translates into pollution patterns that visibly impair air quality, for example. This is true also of the greenhouse gas emissions of these emerging economies, which have dramatically increased in the meantime.

This changed outlook has obviously influenced the global debate. The US has made it clear that it will not join commitments that do not include China, now the world's largest emitter of greenhouse gases. For Europeans, this only underlines the logic of their preference for multilateralism. At the same time, emerging economies feel that their importance is not adequately acknowledged in the structures of the UN, which too much reflects the post-1945 balance of power. And, on top of that, the environmental agenda is perceived by these emerging economies as a potential brake on their development, and so is met with some suspicion just as they start enjoying the fruits of general economic progress.

> Conclusion: the EU remains deeply attached to its tradition of multilateralism, and prefers global environmental problems to be tackled at UN level.

The environment: a new policy area for the EU

EU climate policy basically started as part of environmental policy, which had a sound legal basis established by the Single European Act, which entered into force in 1987. Through that Act, new provisions were added to the EU Treaty dealing with the environment.[6] These provided that the Council (i.e. representatives of the EU Member States) could, together with the European Parliament, decide upon environmental laws on the basis of qualified majority, a provision that is now called the 'ordinary legislative procedure'. Today, 25 years later, there is almost a complete set of EU legislation addressing environmental protection of air quality, water, waste and biodiversity.

With hindsight it is not surprising that decisions on environmental policy were pushed to the European level. Often, countries face similar problems, and pollution often extends beyond borders. For example, discharges into the Rhine, the Meuse or the Danube rivers, may cause pollution in another country further downstream. The same goes for air pollution, as was clearly demonstrated in the 1980s by 'acid rain' caused by UK coal-fired power stations damaging forests and lakes in Scandinavia. As concerns about climate change emerged, it was immediately recognised that the actions of one country affected all others, and the effects too, were often trans-boundary. In addition, it became quickly clear that the EU needed to speak with one voice at international negotiations.

Moreover, the development of the EU's Single Market for goods and services accelerated in the 1980s and 1990s. More competition between products and services produced in different Member States provoked questions about short-term distortions of competition as a result of environmental policy measures developed at Member State level. The institutional move embodied in the Single European Act reflected a general opinion that it would be better that the EU adopt rules to protect the environment at European level, thereby minimising the risk of distortions of competition with the EU's internal market.

In the years following implementation of the new institutional provisions, a debate unfolded as to which kind of instruments were the best to use. In particular, the question was raised whether the policy mix should be widened to include economic instruments.[7] A long and comprehensive debate took place on 'pricing the economic externality' and how to put this into practice. Prices are a very effective way of transmitting information through the economy and influencing behaviour, right down to the levels of individual producers and consumers. This can be achieved through taxes or, alternatively, through the setting of overall limits on pollution levels ('a cap'). In other words, economic instruments can work either directly through setting prices for polluting (e.g. through taxes) or through defining quantities of pollution allowed (e.g. through capping pollution levels).

In the 1990s, the favoured way for pricing was through taxes. Already in 1992, the Commission made a proposal for a combined carbon and energy tax. This led to controversy in the Council and Parliament, the main question being whether adoption was to be done through unanimity (where all Member States have to agree, for example as applied in matters of taxation) or through qualified majority voting (where the Member States have votes weighted according to their size, as applied to matters related to the environment). In the end, after almost a decade of difficult negotiations, the tax route was abandoned at the European level, in particular due to the reservations by some Member States, such as the UK, in giving supranational EU institutions a say over the taxation policies of Member States.

The debate on economic instruments at EU level shifted to cap-setting and emissions trading. The US introduced into the international debate on climate change the advantages that an instrument such as 'cap-and-trade' could bring in fostering the overall cost-effectiveness of policy solutions. Led by their successful policy experience on reducing sulphur and NO_x emissions, the US pushed successfully for its introduction into the Kyoto Protocol, much to the irritation of the Europeans at the time. It took a while before the Europeans appreciated that setting a limit on the total amount of emissions is truly an environmental benefit. Moreover, the EU gradually realised that legislation for such instruments could be decided through Council qualified majority voting, a welcome difference after the institutional stalemate that had stymied progress on carbon and energy taxation.

Conclusion: since the Treaty change of 1987, the EU decides legislation in the field of the environment on the basis of a qualified majority voting of Member States with the European Parliament. This has allowed for the development of a comprehensive set of new environmental legislation and facilitated a smooth policy response towards climate change.

Facts and figures on EU greenhouse gases

The development of new policy instruments such as those on carbon pricing led to a whole new set of policy questions. Are the facts and figures available? What would the estimated economic impact be on important sectors, not least on the energy sector or on the manufacturing industry? Could estimations be undertaken of related costs of emission reductions? These questions had been uncommon in the development of environmental policy until then.

One of the first policy decisions was to create a much better statistical information system through the systematic monitoring, reporting and verification of greenhouse gas emissions in the Member States and in the different economic sectors. Today, the EU's Monitoring Mechanism Regulation[8] is one of the best developed tools worldwide, delivering in the autumn of every year a comprehensive report (EEA, 2014). The availability of solid statistical information is still one of the essential foundations of EU climate policy.

Over the period 1990–2012, the EU's greenhouse gas emissions decreased in all main emitting sectors except transport. Overall emissions (of the 28 Member States) were reduced from 5.6 billion tonnes of CO_2-equivalent in 1990 to 4.6 billion tonnes in 2013. In fact, overall emissions decreased by 19% while the GDP of the EU economy grew by 44% to 2014 (Figure 1.2).

As a result of this successful decoupling, the greenhouse gas emissions' intensity of the EU was reduced by almost half between 1990 and 2012. While emissions decline more in absolute terms at times of low economic growth, the persistent reduction of greenhouse gas intensity over more than two decades demonstrates that progress in terms of decoupling is being made irrespective of economic cycles. Decoupling occurred in all Member States, even while the population increased. Similarly, energy consumption (gross final energy consumption) peaked around 2005 and in 2012 was only 1% above 1990 levels.

The structural policies implemented in the field of climate and energy (see Chapters 2–4) have contributed significantly to the EU emission reduction observed since 2005. A detailed analysis of the reduction in CO_2 emissions from fossil fuel combustion between 2005 and 2012 is shown in Figure 1.3.

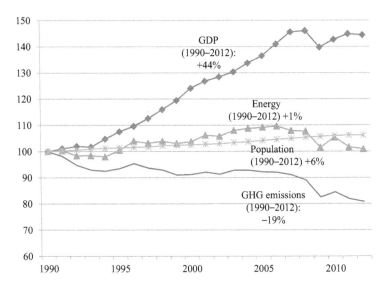

FIGURE 1.2 Greenhouse gases, energy use, population and GDP in the EU-28: 1990–2012 (Index 1990=100)

Sources: EEA (2014a), EEA inventory database, European Commission (Ameco database); data to 2012 (latest inventory data).

Between 2005 and 2008 CO_2 emissions from fossil fuel combustion decreased by 3.4%. This result was the sum of increases caused by population and GDP *per capita* growth, on the one hand, and improvements in energy intensity and carbon intensity, on the other hand. Between 2008 and 2012, CO_2 emissions from fossil fuel combustion fell by 9.2%. This reduction was the sum of an increase caused by population growth, decreases caused by a decline in GDP *per capita*, improvements in energy intensity of GDP and also of carbon intensity per unit of energy produced (see EEA, 2014a).[9] This indicates, significantly, that the economic crisis that occurred during the 2008–2012 period contributed to less than half of the reduction of emissions observed during this period.

The EU's share of global emissions is falling as Europe reduces its own emissions and those from other parts of the world, especially the major emerging economies, are growing rapidly (Table 1.1). The G20 together was responsible for three quarters of global greenhouse gas emissions in 2012. The EU share in global emissions was less than 9% in 2012. China's share increased to 25% in 2012, followed by the US (11%) and Brazil (6%). In 2013, total greenhouse gas emissions *per capita* were 7.3 tonnes CO_2-equivalent in the EU, similar to China. In 2013 *per capita* emissions were highest in Australia and the US compared to the global average. Levels in India, Indonesia and Brazil were much lower.

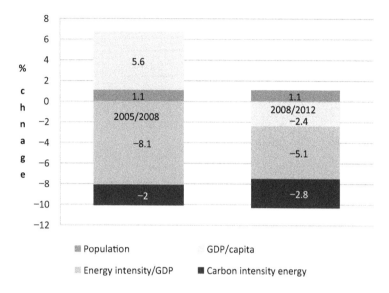

FIGURE 1.3 Why the EU's CO_2 emissions from fossil fuel combustion changed between 2005 and 2012
Source: adapted from EEA (2014a).

TABLE 1.1 Global greenhouse gas emissions since 1990 per country and *capita* (all sources and sinks excluding forest and peat fires)

	Greenhouse gas emissions			Emissions/capita	
	1990 levels	2012 levels	2012 share	1990	2013
	$MtCO_2eq.$		%	$tCO_2/capita$	
World total or average	36,244	49,793	100	4.3	4.9
EU-28	5,368	4,241	8.5	9.2	7.3
US	5,402	5,546	11.1	20	17
China	3,893	12,455	25.0	2.1	7.4
India	1,387	3,003	6.0	0.8	1.7
Japan	1,168	1,268	2.5	9.5	11
Russian Fed.	3,532	1,755	3.5	17	13
Brazil	1,606	2,989	6.0	1.5	2.6
Rep. Korea	301	669	1.3	5.9	13
Mexico	494	663	1.3	3.6	3.9
Canada	520	739	1.5	16	16
Indonesia	1,165	1,171	2.4	0.9	2
Turkey	144	380	0.8	2.8	4.4

(*Continued*)

TABLE 1.1 (Continued)

	Greenhouse gas emissions			Emissions/capita	
	1990 levels	2012 levels	2012 share	1990	2013
	MtCO$_2$eq.		%	tCO$_2$/capita	
Australia	545	559	1.1	16	17
Argentina	267	380	0.8	3.3	4.5
Saudi Arabia	205	549	1.0	10	17
South Africa	349	451	0.9	7.3	6.2
G20 aggregate	26,347	36,819	73.7	n.a.	n.a.

Source: European Commission (2015).

Limiting global warming to 2°C requires a significant reduction in the emissions of greenhouse gases. The largest component is carbon dioxide (CO_2), which in the EU represents more than 80% of total emissions. The release of CO_2 is directly connected with the use of fossil fuels that we use massively in power generation, industry and transport. The other gases are methane (CH_4), nitrous oxide (N_2O) and fluorinated gases (F-gases). These are quantitatively less voluminous, but are more potent global warming gases than CO_2, having a correspondingly greater impact on the climate system.

Figure 1.4 shows the contribution made by the various sectors and gases in 2012. Clearly, CO_2 emissions are the most important and more than 94% of CO_2 emissions come from energy consumption. The second most important gas is methane (CH_4) followed by nitrous oxide (N_2O) and fluorinated gases (F-gases), the latter from industrial processes such as cooling and refrigeration.

Figure 1.5 shows the changes for the various sectors over time. Compared to the EU-wide reduction of 19% in the 1990–2012 period, most sectors have achieved more than this with the exception of the transport sector, where emissions have increased since 1990. Emissions from waste, energy use and industrial processes have, by contrast, fallen by considerably more than the 19% average.

Under the Kyoto Protocol, the 15 countries which were EU Member States in 1997 (the 'EU-15') agreed to reduce their collective emissions of six greenhouse gases in the 2008–2012 period by 8% below 1990 levels. Over the period, these Member States substantially overachieved this target and actually reduced their emissions by as much as 18.5%.

The latest available projections indicate that the trend observed in Figure 1.2 will continue. With current legislation in place, energy consumption

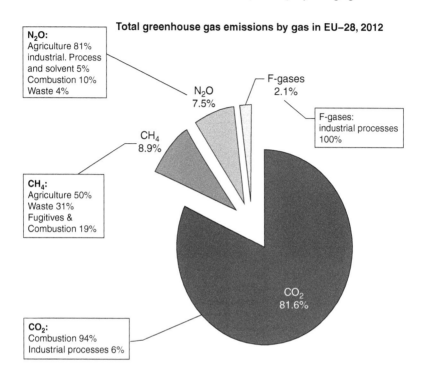

FIGURE 1.4 Total greenhouse gas emissions by gas in the EU-28 in 2012
Source: EEA.

is expected to continue to decrease through to 2035 (Capros et al., 2014). Assuming legislation on renewable energy, energy efficiency and greenhouse gas emissions is successfully implemented, total greenhouse gas emissions are expected to be 23% below 1990 levels in 2020. This would again represent an overachievement of the commitment of 20% that was taken by the EU under the second commitment period of the Kyoto Protocol ending in 2020.

The amount of carbon that is estimated to be stored in the EU's forests and agriculture is not included in the above estimates. In the EU the amount of carbon of the Land Use, Land-Use Change and Forestry (LULUCF) sector has been more or less stable: the carbon 'sink', which is carbon fixed in soil and vegetation, was estimated at around 288 million tonnes of CO_2-equivalent in 2000 and at 296 million tonnes of CO_2-equivalent in 2010, but the datasets on which estimates are based are incomplete and uncertainties are high.

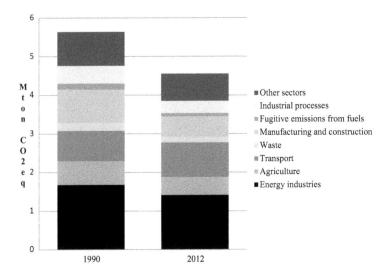

FIGURE 1.5 Changes in EU-28 greenhouse gas emissions by sector, 1990–2012
Sources: based on EEA (2014) and EEA data viewer consulted 18.3.2015 (www.eea.europa.eu/
data-and-maps/data/data-viewers/greenhouse-gases-viewer).

Conclusion: the EU has succeeded in decoupling its emissions from economic growth. Since 1990 GDP increased by 45% (to 2013) while emissions decreased by 19%. At the same time the obligations under the Kyoto Protocol to 2012 were achieved and surpassed: a reduction of 8% was promised; a reduction of 18% was delivered. Also for 2020 an overachievement is likely.

Implementation of the 2020 climate and energy package

On the basis of the Commission's proposal, the March 2007 European Council made an independent commitment to reduce overall greenhouse gas emissions by 20% compared to 1990 levels.

'Independent' meant that the EU would implement the emission reduction commitment irrespective of what other countries would do in terms of reducing greenhouse gas emissions. This commitment was part of a broader climate and energy strategy, aimed at creating a competitive edge in emerging new technologies, and reducing economic vulnerability against rising import prices for fossil fuels, and more generally for energy security reasons. The greenhouse gas reduction commitment was therefore accompanied by specific energy objectives, notably a binding target to increase the share of renewable energy in final energy consumption to 20% in 2020 (from about 8.5% in 2005), and an indicative target to reduce energy consumption by 20% in 2020.[10]

The 20% greenhouse gas reduction commitment[11] was embodied in a package of legislative measures that were all agreed by the EU before the Copenhagen Conference of Parties to the UNFCCC in December 2009. The underlying rationale for doing this was to show the EU's seriousness of intent and commitment to the international negotiations.

These legislative initiatives were collectively called the 'climate and energy package', and consisted of six pieces of legislation that were all finally adopted in April 2009:

1   Directive 2009/29/EC of the European Parliament and of the Council of 23 April 2009 amending Directive 2003/87/EC so as to improve and extend the greenhouse gas emission allowance trading scheme of the Community.[12]

2   Decision No. 406/2009/EC of the European Parliament and of the Council of 23 April 2009 on the effort of Member States to reduce their greenhouse gas emissions to meet the Community's greenhouse gas emission reduction commitments up to 2020, hereafter referred to as the Effort Sharing Decision.[13]

3   Directive 2009/28/EC of the European Parliament and of the Council of 23 April 2009 on the promotion of the use of energy from renewable sources and amending and subsequently repealing Directives 2001/77/EC and 2003/30/EC.[14]

4   Directive 2009/30/EC of the European Parliament and of the Council of 23 April 2009 amending Directive 98/70/EC as regards the specification of petrol, diesel and gas-oil and introducing a mechanism to monitor and reduce greenhouse gas emissions and amending Council Directive 1999/32/EC as regards the specification of fuel used by inland waterway vessels.[15]

5   Regulation (EC) No. 443/2009 of the European Parliament and of the Council of 23 April 2009 setting emission performance standards for new passenger cars as part of the Community's integrated approach to reduce CO_2 emissions from light-duty vehicles.[16]

6   Directive 2009/31/EC of the European Parliament and of the Council of 23 April 2009 on the geological storage of carbon dioxide.[17]

To meet the 20% reduction target in greenhouse gas emissions it was decided that the sources covered by the EU's Emissions Trading System (ETS) should reduce their greenhouse gas emissions by 21% compared to 2005. The year 2005 was chosen since it was the first year for which verified emissions data for the installations covered by the ETS were available.

Other emissions sources, not covered by the ETS (e.g. transport, buildings, the services sector, small industries and agriculture), but covered by the Effort Sharing Decision, had to reduce their collective emissions by 10% compared to 2005. The split between reductions to be delivered by ETS versus the sectors not covered by the ETS was based on economic analysis showing that it would be relatively cheaper to reduce emissions in the ETS sectors than in the non-ETS sectors. In other words, for the same marginal costs (or carbon price) more reduction would be achieved in the ETS than in the non-ETS.

A major issue in the negotiations leading to adoption of the package was the distribution of effort, and hence costs, across Member States. The economic analysis underpinning the package had demonstrated considerable differences in costs if effort (and targets) would be distributed purely on the basis of cost-effectiveness (i.e. an equal marginal cost of abatement per Member State). Cost-effectiveness alone would mean that lower-income Member States, notably in Eastern Europe, would be facing relatively higher costs in relative terms, because of their relatively higher energy- and carbon-intensity and because of their relatively lower GDP. At the same time, it was crucial to ensure cost-effectiveness, as the costs of compliance could rise sharply if low-cost abatement options, for instance in old and inefficient power and industrial plants in Eastern Europe, were not realised.

The architecture of the package therefore had to engineer a smart combination of *targets*, on the one hand, that were differentiated to reflect fairness and solidarity, and *policy instruments* on the other hand, that ensure a cost-effective implementation.

The principle of using cost-effective policy instruments is exemplified by the use of the EU ETS as an EU-wide market-based instrument, covering more than 11,000 power and industrial installations across Europe, with one EU-wide cap on emissions (rather than distinct national targets for ETS-covered sectors). Such an EU-wide approach ensures that abatement is achieved where cheapest and avoids distortion of competition between large industrial installations within the EU. Similarly, EU-wide energy- or CO_2-efficiency standards for cars and products are based on internal market principles, given that these goods can be freely traded across the EU, and thereby enable the harnessing of economies of scale provided by a market of more than 500 million consumers.

The principle of ensuring a fair distribution of the effort was achieved in several ways. First, in the EU ETS, this was accomplished through a redistribution of allowances for auctioning (as explained in more detail in Chapter 2), thereby ensuring a redistribution of the revenues that each Member State could expect. In other words, the burden-sharing as agreed in the Council for the first commitment period of the Kyoto Protocol was replaced, at least for the sectors covered by the EU ETS, by a fully harmonised policy instrument with a sharing of auctioning revenues.

Second, when setting emissions targets for each Member State in sectors not covered by the EU ETS (notably transport, buildings, agriculture and smaller businesses), account was taken of the national *per capita* income,[18] leading to the differentiated targets for each Member State of the Effort Sharing Decision, ranging from −20% compared to 2005 for the highest income countries to +20% compared to 2005 for countries with the lowest average *per capita* income (see Delbeke et al., 2010; Capros et al., 2011). In this way, Member States with similar economic performance, often neighbouring each other, were allocated similar targets. This approach greatly facilitated agreement in the Council.

Considering the uncertainties related to future economic development, and to enhance cost-effective achievement of targets, further flexibility was also introduced between Member States in the Effort Sharing Decision, allowing the transfer of emission rights between them. In this way, countries facing higher costs could achieve their target more cheaply, and countries overachieving their target could be financially rewarded. Finally, in both the ETS and the Effort Sharing Decision a limited amount of international credits were allowed to be used.

Conclusion: the EU adopted for 2020 a set of targets for climate and energy: 20% greenhouse gas reduction, 20% renewable energy, and 20% energy efficiency improvement. An integrated approach, with the flexibilities foreseen in each of the instruments, allows the targets to be met in a cost-effective manner, while sharing the burden between Member States on the basis of their relative wealth.

The road to 2050 and the new targets for 2030

The EU has repeatedly confirmed its commitment to the below-2°C objective, as well as to the long-term target this requires, i.e. a 80–95% reduction of greenhouse gases by 2050 compared to 1990. But questions still remained on the reduction pathways and on the technological, behavioural and energy and transport-system changes that such a major transition to a low-carbon economy implies over time.

In 2011, the European Commission therefore produced a Low Carbon Roadmap and an Energy Roadmap to flesh out the perspective through to 2050.[19] The objective of this exercise was not to try to forecast the likely economic, technological and societal changes over such a long timeframe, but rather to deepen the understanding and provide more underlying analysis regarding questions such as:

- What is the domestic greenhouse gas reduction the EU needs to achieve as part of a low-carbon transition consistent with the below-2°C objective?
- What is the cost-efficient pathway towards 2050, and what are the milestones for 2030, 2040 and 2050? What does this pathway look like for key sectors such as power generation, transport, industry, buildings and agriculture? What is the range of the expected costs and benefits?
- Can we afford to delay action until, perhaps, more technologies are available? What are the key technologies that are crucially important in the low-carbon transition and which therefore require important R&D efforts? What is the impact of early availability or non-availability of certain technologies (nuclear, Carbon Capture and Storage (CCS), energy storage, electrification of transport)?
- Can we make estimates of the investment needs, and in how far that is balanced through reduced energy bills?
- How does the energy mix evolve? What is the role of gas in the transition? Is it feasible to have very high levels of variable renewables (wind, solar) and, if so, what are the implications for the electricity system? What is the impact of a global energy transition on fossil fuel prices and hence on the policies needed to achieve such a pathway?
- What might be the role of biomass or biofuels considering potential global land-use constraints, such as the need to stop deforestation?
- What does decarbonisation imply for energy-intensive industrial sectors?

The low-carbon economy 2050 Roadmap was based primarily on economic and cost-effectiveness considerations. It showed that, as part of a global effort to meet 2°C, it is technologically and economically feasible for the EU to achieve *domestic* emission reductions of at least 80% compared to 1990 in 2050. In this way, the 2050 Roadmap made clear that making use of international offset credits could not be the main instrument to achieve deep emission reductions in the order of 80–95%.

The Roadmap also sets out interim reductions, so called 'milestones', of 40% by 2030 and 60% by 2040. It also elaborates how the main sectors (power generation, industry, transport, buildings and construction, as well as agriculture) could make the transition to a low-carbon economy cost-effectively (see Figure 1.6).[20] These pathways are quite different for the different sectors, in terms of scale and pace. The analysis done showed, for example, that the pace of the transition was the fastest in power generation, enabled through a mix of comparatively low-cost low-carbon technologies. In buildings, substantial progress is also possible through sustained efforts to construct new low-energy houses, deep renovation of existing buildings and increased efficiency of heating and cooling systems.

Transport and industry also show moderate reductions until 2030, mostly through efficiency improvements. However, after 2030, innovative technologies would be needed, such as the deployment of electric mobility and CCS. Finally, agricultural emissions are the ones that are reduced the least. This is in large part due to the fact that these emissions are closely linked to meat consumption, and hence further reductions would require behavioural changes of diet.

An important finding of the low-carbon economy 2050 Roadmap relates to investment needs. To make this transition, it was estimated that the EU would need to invest an additional €270 billion, or 1.5% of its GDP annually, on average, over the period 2010–2050, over and above investments that would be needed anyway. These are largely investments in capital goods,

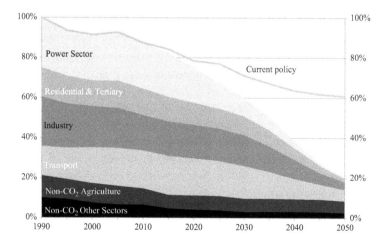

FIGURE 1.6 The transition to a low-carbon EU economy in 2050 (greenhouse gas emissions by sector over time as % of 1990 levels

such as low-carbon generation technologies (e.g. solar, on and offshore wind, nuclear, CCS), extended grid connections, including smart grids, new automotive and other transport technologies, low-energy houses, more efficient appliances, etc.

The development and production of these kinds of products and equipment are one of the strengths of Europe's economy. The low-carbon transition therefore provides a major opportunity for Europe's manufacturing industry, provided it succeeds in maintaining and enhancing its technological edge. No longer blessed with major natural resources and confronted with higher labour costs, innovation is clearly one of the major industrial policy directions needed for the EU to create more economic growth and new jobs. In addition, the EU would become less dependent on expensive imports of oil and gas and less vulnerable to increases in oil prices. On average, and subject to the uncertainties of future oil prices, the EU could save between €175–320 billion annually in fuel costs over the next 40 years.

Furthermore, greater use of clean technologies and electric cars is expected to substantially reduce air pollution in European cities. Fewer people would suffer from asthma and other respiratory diseases, and mortality would decline. Considerably less money would need to be spent on equipment to control air pollution and significant monetary benefits would accrue from, for example, reduced mortality. By 2050, the EU could save up to €88 billion a year in respect of air quality benefits.

Building on these discussions the Commission published a Communication entitled *A policy framework for climate and energy policies in the period from 2020 to 2030*.[21] It concentrated on the opportunities and challenges for 2030 and outlined the questions for a debate by Heads of State and Government.

In October 2014, the European Council adopted a series of targets in view of 2030: at least 40% domestic greenhouse gas reduction target (below 1990 levels), of 'at least 27%' for renewable energy 'binding at EU level', and an 'indicative target' of 'at least 27%' for energy efficiency.[22] An additional objective of 'arriving at a 15% target by 2030' with respect to interconnectivity in electricity networks between Member States was also agreed, reflecting the crucial role of electricity connectors to strengthen the EU internal market for electricity, to enable greater penetration of renewable energy and to improve security of supply.

It was further agreed that the reduction factor of the EU ETS would be increased from 1.74% per year at present to 2.2% per year from 2021. This would equate to a reduction of emissions from the EU ETS sectors of 43% compared to their level in 2005. For the sectors not covered by the ETS, a reduction of emissions of 30% compared to 2005 was agreed and would be differentiated among Member States between 0% and −40% (compared to

2005). Further elements were agreed ensuring fairness between the Member States, as well as provisions to limit 'carbon leakage' (i.e. the shifting of production and emissions outside the EU) resulting from third country competition.

For renewable energy a target at EU level was agreed without explicit differentiation between Member States. No sub-target was set for transport, unlike for 2020, reflecting the wish of Member States for greater flexibility. At the same time, the European Council suggested a strengthened role of the EU ETS in spurring the deployment of mature renewable technologies, and a strengthened role for the EU to ensure that the target is met collectively. All of this implies that a revision of the Directive on renewable energy is necessary for the period after 2020.

Energy efficiency will continue to play an important role in meeting all objectives of EU energy policy. The indicative target of 'at least 27%' will enhance energy supply security and is expected to stimulate investments in buildings as well as in new technologies. It will contribute to growth and jobs while limiting energy bills for consumers.[23]

Important to note is that the European Council reaffirmed the central role of the EU ETS as a key instrument to reduce greenhouse gas emissions in the covered sectors. It further acknowledged the importance of 'an instrument to stabilise the market in line with the Commission proposal' for a Market Stability Reserve[24] to address the significant surplus of allowances in the EU ETS. In May 2015 negotiations on this were still not formally finalised between the European Parliament and the Council, although a political agreement had been reached. Once operating, the Market Stability Reserve will automatically adjust the volumes of allowances to be auctioned in accordance with predefined and transparent rules. As such, this proposal will enhance the resilience of the EU ETS in the case of unexpected increases or decreases in the number of allowances in the market.

Conclusion: the EU has taken up the challenge to limit climate change to 2°C. This requires a domestic emission reduction of at least 80% by 2050. Today the 20% target for 2020 has almost been achieved and a political commitment at the highest political level has been made for a domestic reduction of (at least) 40% by 2030. The EU has based its policy on considerations related to cost-effectiveness and relies on market-based instruments. Through more than a decade of continued policy along those lines, the EU has assumed leadership in the development and deployment of low-carbon technology.

Notes

1 Hansen, J. (2012) 'Why I must speak out about climate change', TED2012 Talk, February 2012 Conference Presentation: www.ted.com/talks/james_hansen_why_i_must_speak_out_about_climate_change
2 Community Strategy on Climate Change – Council Conclusions, paragraph 6: http://europa.eu/rapid/press-release_PRES-96–188_en.htm?locale=en
3 See paragraph 27 of Brussels European Council Conclusions of 8–9 March 2007 (document reference: 7224/1/07 REV 1 dated 2 May 2007): www.consilium.europa.eu/uedocs/cms_data/docs/pressdata/en/ec/93135.pdf
4 Climate Summit 2014, Chair's Summary: 'Leaders committed to limit global temperature rise to less than 2 degrees Celsius from pre-industrial levels': www.un.org/climatechange/summit/2014/09/2014-climate-change-summary-chairs-summary
5 Submission by Latvia and the European Commission on behalf of the European Union and its Member States, dated 6 March 2015, on the Intended Nationally Determined Contribution of the EU and its Member States: http://ec.europa.eu/clima/news/docs/2015030601_eu_indc_en.pdf
6 Now Part 3, Title XX of the Treaty on the Functioning of the European Union, OJ C 326, 26.10.2012, pp. 132–134: http://eur-lex.europa.eu/legal-content/EN/TXT/PDF/?uri=CELEX:12012E/TXT&from=en
7 European Commission (1993) White Paper 'Growth, competitiveness, employment: The challenges and ways forward into the 21st century' COM(1993) 700 of 5 December 1993, pp. 140–151: http://europa.eu/documentation/official-docs/white-papers/pdf/growth_wp_com_93_700_parts_a_b.pdf
8 Regulation (EU) No. 525/2013 of the European Parliament and of the Council of 21 May 2013 on a mechanism for monitoring and reporting greenhouse gas emissions and for reporting other information at national and Union level relevant to climate change and repealing Decision No. 280/2004/EC; OJ L 165, 18.6.2013, pp. 13–40: http://eur-lex.europa.eu/legal-content/EN/TXT/PDF/?uri=CELEX:32013R0525&from=EN
9 European Commission (2014) 'Progress towards achieving the Kyoto and EU 2020 objectives', Brussels (COM(2014) 689 final, dated 28 October 2014): http://ec.europa.eu/transparency/regdoc/rep/1/2014/EN/1–2014–689-EN-F1–1.Pdf. The figure is based on analysis of the EEA (2014a) 'Why did greenhouse gas emissions decrease in the EU in 2012?' European Environment Agency – EEA Analysis, Copenhagen, 3 June 2014 (www.eea.europa.eu/publications/why-did-ghg-emissions-decrease).
10 Compared to the EU's projected energy consumption in 2020, as established in the 2007 baseline scenario of the Impact Assessment for the 2020 climate and energy package (see Capros et al., 2008).
11 The 20% reduction in greenhouse gas emissions compared to 2020 is equivalent to an emission reduction of 14% compared to 2005.
12 OJ L 140, 5.6.2009, pp. 63–87; http://eur-lex.europa.eu/LexUriServ/LexUriServ.do?uri=OJ:L:2009:140:0063:0087:en:PDF
13 OJ L 140, 5.6.2009, pp. 136–148; http://eur-lex.europa.eu/LexUriServ/LexUriServ.do?uri=OJ:L:2009:140:0136:0148:EN:PDF

14 OJ L 140, 5.6.2009, pp. 16–62; http://eur-lex.europa.eu/legal-content/EN/TXT/PDF/?uri=CELEX:32009L0028&from=en

15 OJ L 140, 5.6.2009, pp. 88–113; http://eur-lex.europa.eu/legal-content/EN/TXT/PDF/?uri=CELEX:32009L0030&from=EN

16 OJ L 140, 5.6.2009, pp. 1–15; http://eur-lex.europa.eu/legal-content/EN/TXT/PDF/?uri=CELEX:32009R0443&from=EN

17 OJ L 140, 5.6.2009, pp. 114–135; http://eur-lex.europa.eu/legal-content/EN/TXT/PDF/?uri=CELEX:32009L0031&from=EN

18 This principle was also used, to some extent, in the definition of the renewable energy targets for each Member State.

19 European Commission (2011) 'A Roadmap for moving to a competitive low carbon economy in 2050', COM(2011) 112 final of 8.3.2011 (http://eur-lex.europa.eu/resource.html?uri=cellar:5db26ecc-ba4e-4de2-ae08-dba649109d18.0002.03/DOC_1&format=PDF) and European Commission (2011) 'Energy Roadmap 2050'
COM(2011) 885 final of 15.12.2011 (http://eur-lex.europa.eu/legal-content/EN/TXT/PDF/?uri=CELEX:52011DC0885&rid=3).

20 European Commission (2011): Communication: 'A Roadmap for moving to a competitive low carbon economy in 2050', COM(2011) 112 final of 8.3.2011(http://eur-lex.europa.eu/resource.html?uri=cellar:5db26ecc-ba4e-4de2-ae08-dba649109d18.0002.03/DOC_1&format=PDF)

21 European Commission (2014) 'A policy framework for climate and energy in the period from 2020 to 2030', COM(2014) 15 final of 22.1.2014. http://eur-lex.europa.eu/legal-content/EN/TXT/PDF/?uri=CELEX:52014DC0015&from=EN

22 European Council 23/24 October 2014, Conclusions. EUCO 169/14. European Council, Brussels, 24 October 2014: www.consilium.europa.eu/uedocs/cms_data/docs/pressdata/en/ec/145397.pdf

23 European Commission (2014) 'Energy efficiency and its contribution to energy security and the 2030 Framework for climate and energy policy', COM(2014) 520 final, 23.7.2014, as well as its accompanying Staff Working Document: http://ec.europa.eu/energy/sites/ener/files/documents/2014_eec_communication_adopted_0.pdf

24 European Commission (2014) 'Proposal for a Decision of the European Parliament and of the Council concerning the establishment and operation of a market stability reserve for the Union greenhouse gas emission trading scheme and amending Directive 2003/87/EC' of 22.1.2014; http://eur-lex.europa.eu/legal-content/EN/TXT/PDF/?uri=CELEX:52014PC0020&from=EN

References

Capros, P.L. Mantzos, Papandreou, V., and Tasios, N. (2008) European Energy and Transport trends to 2030 – update 2007. Publications Office of the European Union, Luxembourg (http://ec.europa.eu/dgs/energy_transport/figures/trends_2030_update_2007/energy_transport_trends_2030_update_2007_en.pdf).

Capros, P., Mantzos, L., Parousos, L., Tasios, N., Klaassen, G., and van Ierland, T. (2011) Analysis of the EU policy package on climate change and renewables. *Energy Policy* 39(3): 1476–1485.

Capros, P., de Vita, A., Tasios, N., Papadopoulos, D., Siskos, P., Apostolaki, E., Zampara, M., Paroussos, L., Fragiadakis, K., Kouvaritakis, N., Hoglund-Isaksson, L., Winiwarter, W., Purohit, P., Böttcher, H., Frank, S., Havlik, P., Gustu, M., and Witzke, H.P. (2014) 'EU energy, transport and GHG emissions: trends to 2050, reference scenario 2013'. Publications office of the European Union, Luxembourg (http://ec.europa.eu/clima/policies/2030/models/eu_trends_2050_en.pdf).

Delbeke, J., Klaassen, G., van Ierland, T., and Zapfel, P. (2010) The Role of Environmental Economics in Recent Policy Making at the European Commission *Review of Environmental Economics and Policy* 4(1): 24–43.

EEA (2014) Annual European Union greenhouse gas inventory 1990–2012 and inventory report 2014, Technical report Submission to the UNFCCC Secretariat, EEA Technical report No. 9/2014, European Environment Agency, Copenhagen (www.eea.europa.eu/publications/european-union-greenhouse-gas-inventory-2014).

EEA (2014a) 'Why did greenhouse gas emissions decrease in the EU in 2012? European Environment Agency – Analysis, Copenhagen' (www.eea.europa.eu/publications/why-did-ghg-emissions-decrease).

European Commission (2015) 'The Paris Protocol – a blueprint for tackling global climate change beyond 2020', Commission Staff Working Document SWD (2015) 17 final of 25 February 2015, Brussels (http://ec.europa.eu/priorities/energy-union/docs/paris-swd_en.pdf).

IPCC (2013) Summary for Policymakers. In: *Climate Change 2013: The Physical Science Basis. Contribution of Working Group I to the Fifth Assessment Report of the Intergovernmental Panel on Climate Change*, Stocker, T.F., Qin, D., Plattner, G.-K., Tignor, M., Allen, S.K., Boschung, J., Nauels, A., Xia, Y., Bex, V and Midgley, P.M. (eds.), Cambridge University Press, Cambridge, United Kingdom and New York, NY, USA, pp. 1–30. doi:10.1017/CBO9781107415324.004 (www.ipcc.ch/pdf/assessment-report/ar5/wg1/WG1AR5_SPM_FINAL.pdf).

IPCC (2014): Climate Change 2014: Synthesis Report. Contribution of Working Groups I, II and III to the Fifth Assessment Report of the Intergovernmental Panel on Climate Change, Core Writing Team, Pachauri, R.K., and Meyer, L.A. (eds.), IPCC, Geneva, Switzerland, 151 pp.

Meadows, D. H., Meadows, D., Randers, J., and Behrens III, W.W. (1972) *Limits to Growth*, New York: Universe Books (www.donellameadows.org/wp-content/userfiles/Limits-to-Growth-digital-scan-version.pdf).

2

EU ETS: PRICING CARBON TO DRIVE COST-EFFECTIVE REDUCTIONS ACROSS EUROPE

Damien Meadows, Yvon Slingenberg and Peter Zapfel

The ETS is the EU's cap-and-trade system for greenhouse gas emissions

The EU ETS covers half of EU emissions

A core element of the EU climate and energy policy since 2005 has been putting a price on greenhouse gas emissions and using market forces to contribute to the necessary emission reductions. The EU Emissions Trading System (ETS), a so-called cap-and-trade system, creates such a price.

Cap-and-trade systems guarantee an environmental outcome by setting a limit ('cap') on the total amount of carbon emissions. Such a system foresees the issuance of allowances in quantities corresponding to the emissions cap, and these allowances are then allocated to companies covered by the system. The trading of these allowances is allowed, while maintaining the obligation that companies covered regularly surrender sufficient allowances to match their actual emissions. The benefit is that it enables reductions in emissions across all the installations covered by the system in the most cost-effective manner. A company will find it in its own interest to cut emissions and sell allowances when the market price for allowances is higher than the costs to reduce its emissions. Conversely, those companies with reduction costs exceeding the market price will prefer to purchase allowances. Reductions are incentivised where costs of abatement are lowest, while the environmental outcome remains guaranteed by the overall emissions ceiling. When a variety of sectors is covered, it allows continued growth for individual sectors by purchasing allowances from other sectors, where emission reductions are cheaper to make.

Cap-and-trade systems, and other market-based measures like carbon taxes, also have the potential to generate money that can be used for climate change mitigation and adaptation. They also strengthen the business case for making investments in low-carbon technology: the rate of return is improved and the payback period is reduced, as compared to more carbon-intensive ones. By putting a price on carbon, companies and economic actors are encouraged to include its value in their operational decision-making and long-term investment planning.

In short, cap-and-trade is a valuable tool because it can reduce greenhouse gas emissions more cost-effectively than other policy options, which means that greater reductions can be achieved for the same cost. In the light of the advantages of this instrument, the EU established the EU ETS, which has been in place since 2005. Some inspiration was found from the solid design of the SO_2 allowance trading system under the US Clean Air Act. For the EU, the choice of this market-based instrument represented a significant departure from previous EU environmental legislation.

The EU has developed the world's first multi-country cap-and-trade scheme for greenhouse gases. It now applies across 31 countries (the 28 EU Member States, Iceland, Liechtenstein and Norway), with a combined population of over 500 million people. The EU ETS applies to more than 12,000 industrial plants and aircraft operators. It covers around half of European CO_2 emissions. It has established a true internal market for carbon allowances. Whether in Bulgaria, Finland or Portugal, the price of pollution is the same and installations are treated in a similar and predictable manner.

A multi-billion euro market

The European carbon market has delivered since its start a very high level of compliance. Figure 2.1 shows the development of annual verified emissions since 2005. Due to the lack of monitoring at installation level and independent verification, no comparable figures exist for the years prior to the introduction of the EU ETS. However, several studies (e.g. Ellerman and Buchner, 2008; Ellerman et al., 2010) point to the fact that the carbon price signal has resulted in real emission reductions since the very beginning of the EU ETS. The largest drop in emissions was experienced between 2008 and 2009, which is to a large extent explained by the onset of the economic crisis in late 2008. So far, however, no robust empirical studies have been carried out to disaggregate various drivers of emission reductions, such as the recession, the impacts of the carbon price and other policies to specifically promote renewables or energy efficiency.

The EU ETS works with the economic cycle: a recession of an average magnitude leads to somewhat lower emissions, affects the supply–demand balance in the carbon market and, therefore causes a lower carbon price. A fluctuating carbon price is a normal feature that does not undermine the overall predictability of the ETS. Furthermore, companies are allowed to bank emission allowances, and so are incentivised to reduce emissions earlier in time and overachieve. While banking was not allowed from the pilot phase of 2005–7 because of its trial nature (which explains the drop in value of 2005–7 allowances by the end of that period), the banking of companies' holdings of allowances without restriction has been the rule from 2008 onwards.

Turning to market activity, available figures (see Figures 2.2 and 2.3) illustrate the impressive growth in both the volume and value of allowances transacted between 2005 and 2012. These figures illustrate that the EU ETS exists not only on paper but that it has given rise over the years to a very actively traded market. It was only the deep recession, and the resulting major price decline, that broke the trend of growing market value between 2005 and 2011, and in 2012 led to a drop in annual market value. At the same time, despite the economic crisis and the much-reduced carbon price, the market volume kept rising in 2012 and 2013 and is expected to increase further.

A well-functioning market requires trust and confidence that all players play by the rules. It is therefore of utmost importance that a solid system of

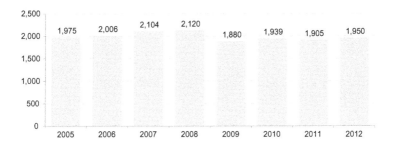

FIGURE 2.1 Annual emissions reported under EU ETS (all figures in million tonnes of carbon dioxide)

Source: Bloomberg New Energy Finance.

Notes: Data refer to Verified Emissions as reported in the EUTL. Data are not on a like-for-like basis and therefore includes emissions from all installations participating in the EU ETS in a given year. Aviation is excluded from 2012 data.

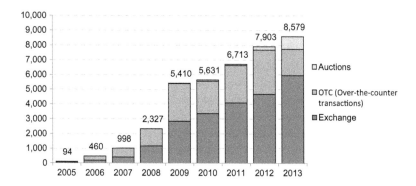

FIGURE 2.2 Annual market volume (all figures in million tonnes of CO_2-equivalent)
Source: Bloomberg New Energy Finance.

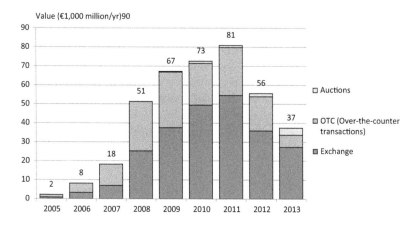

FIGURE 2.3 Annual market value (all figures in €1,000 million)
Sources: Data from Bloomberg, ICE, Bluenext, EEX, GreenX, Climex, CCX, Greenmarket, Nordpool; other sources include UNFCCC and Bloomberg New Energy Finance estimations.

monitoring, reporting and verification of emissions is in place. Similarly, there have to be effective compliance provisions. Since 2008 in the EU ETS, in case of failure to comply, there is a penalty of €100 per tonne of excess emission plus the obligation to make up the shortfall.

Conclusion: the EU ETS covers half of the EU's CO_2 emissions, mainly from the power sector and manufacturing industry. It represents current emissions of a little less than 2 billion tonnes of CO_2, and this amount is declining gradually over time. Market value was climbing to some €80 billion in 2011, but fell back to some €50 billion in 2013, following the protracted economic downturn in Europe.

Key design elements

The central role of a binding emissions cap

A binding, enforceable and decreasing cap placed on absolute greenhouse gas emissions is a core principle of the EU ETS. This is simple, clear and has significant advantages over alternative approaches such as setting targets based on expectations of future emissions growth, or compared to the relative efficiency of particular processes or production techniques. Within this overall limit, individual companies have the freedom to reduce or increase emissions as they see fit, and the system will ensure that the overall cap is met.

The overall cap for the EU ETS has been calculated to correspond with what economic analysis has shown would be a cost-effective contribution from the sectors covered to meeting the EU's overall economy-wide 20% greenhouse gas reduction commitment for 2020. The cap decreases by 1.74% per year from 2010 based on the average cap for 2008–12, the second phase of the EU ETS.[1] This annual reduction factor of 1.74% has been fixed in order to reach an annual amount of carbon allowances 21% below 2005[2] levels by 2020.

The cap continues to reduce after 2020, although as mentioned in Chapter 1, the European Council has agreed that the reduction factor be increased to 2.2% a year from 2021, in order that a 43% reduction be attained by the ETS sectors by 2030 compared to 2005. These respective shares are determined by what is estimated to be a cost-effective contribution by the sectors covered to meet a 40% economy-wide target by 2030.

The progressively tighter, legally binding cap on emissions applies at an overall level, not at company level. Four months after the end of each calendar year, each company must surrender sufficient allowances to cover its entire emissions for the previous year, or financial penalties apply.

> Conclusion: a clear and predictable decline of the cap over a long period of time is a core design feature of the EU ETS. The total amount of allowances is being reduced annually at a rate of 1.74% until 2020, and by 2.2% as of 2021.

More than half of carbon allowances are auctioned

There is a choice when setting up an emissions trading system as to whether allowances are given away for free or not. The political decision when setting up the system in 2005 was for the majority of allowances to be given out for free. From 2013 onwards, about half of the allowances are being auctioned, primarily to the power sector.

It is important to note that an emissions trading system is intended to have price effects that flow through supply chains to the final consumer. There have been several studies on when and to what extent these signals are passed through (Sijm et al., 2008; Alexeeva-Talebi, 2010; Lise et al., 2010; Solier and Jouvet, 2013). In this context, there has been much discussion on the question of whether companies were making additional profits by passing through to consumers the price of allowances that they received for free (so-called 'windfall profits'). This has been particularly highlighted in relation to the power sector, and for that reason no free allocation is given to the power sector from 2013, except for some investment support in eight Member States.

The decisions taken to avoid 'windfall profits' does not affect the environmental outcome of the EU ETS, but their political importance must not be underestimated. It should also be noted that, alongside the encouragement that the EU ETS gives for emission reductions, the value of free allocations can help companies with investment costs for equipment to make emission reductions. For example, the technology to gasify paper-industry waste products into biofuel costs more than twice as much as a standard boiler, and the value of allowances can help pay for such capital investments.

The EU ETS has seen an evolution from individual Member State initially selling very limited amounts of allowances by auction, to an EU-wide auctioning process using a common auction platform in which almost all Member States participate. The legislation states that auctions shall be designed to ensure that operators have full, fair and equitable access, that all participants have access to the same information at the same time, that access to allowances is granted for small emitters and that the organisation and participation in auctions is cost-efficient. The Auctioning Regulation adopted in 2010 fixes the auctioning rules in detail.

From a European perspective, it makes sense to have one single platform, a single regime where everyone can have equal access. The European Energy Exchange (EEX) based in Leipzig has been carrying out the role of the EU ETS's common auction platform on behalf of 25 Member States, after selection through a joint procurement exercise. Germany, the UK and Poland opted out of the common platform and have parallel auction platforms or arrangements.

The EU itself has also been involved in the sale of allowances, through a provision of the Directive which earmarks the value of up to 300 million allowances for investment in the commercial demonstration of specific technologies for reducing emissions, in particular for Carbon Capture and Storage (CCS) plants and large-scale demonstration of innovative renewable energy technologies. This provision is administered through a fund called the 'NER300', which refers to the New Entrant Reserve from which 300 million allowances were reserved for this purpose. Acting through the European Investment Bank (EIB), around €2 billion has been raised from selling these allowances. This is of particular relevance because the EU ETS carbon price is intended to stimulate the lowest-cost emission reductions, and therefore does not directly promote pre-commercial demonstration of promising technologies which have higher costs than the prevailing carbon price. The NER300 proceeds have been used to co-finance a number of development and demonstration projects.[3]

In addition, the legislation[4] allows conditional free allocation for modernisation of the power sector. Eight of the Member States that joined the EU in 2004 have taken up this option and submitted plans to the European Commission on how these free allocations will be linked to commitments from private companies for investments to modernise the power sector. Conditional allocations worth the value of around 680 million allowances are to be invested in the modernisation of their power sectors up to 2019.

Aside from a limited earmarking of revenues at EU level for CCS and renewables under the NER300, it is important to note that the majority of money generated from auctions is in the control of Member States. European legislation states that at least half of auction revenues *should* be used by Member States to tackle climate change, and a Declaration by Heads of State emphasises Member States' willingness to do this.[5] A first official reporting by Member States shows that over €3 billion of auctioning revenues in 2013 is intended to be used for supporting internal and external climate policies.[6]

Finally, it is also important to note that auction revenue is, to an extent, redistributed across the EU to reflect equity and solidarity. Of these allowances, 88% to be auctioned are distributed among Member States based on their historical share of verified emissions, while 10% is distributed among certain Member States for the purpose of solidarity and growth and, up to 2020, a further 2% distributed among Member States whose emissions were at least 20% below their Kyoto Protocol base-year emissions in 2005.[7]

This distributional element in a multi-country context was instrumental in mobilising support for the legislation and is a valuable tool – like free allowances for companies – to gain political acceptability for a cap-and-trade system while preserving an efficient market outcome. This worked out well for the 2020 targets. Similar distributional elements have been of key importance to the adoption of the 2030 package. While the 10% distribution was kept, the 2% element was substituted in favour of a modernisation fund that will facilitate the modernisation of the power sector in Member States with a GDP *per capita* significantly below the EU average.

Conclusion: of the allowances issued, more than half are being auctioned according to strict market rules, primarily to the power sector.

A considerable proportion of carbon allowances are given out for free

Almost half of the allowances under the EU ETS are given out for free from 2013 onwards, the majority of these to industrial activities. While in a perfect world economists would advise that all allowances should be auctioned, this is not quite the case where all major economies are not pricing the external costs of greenhouse gas emissions to an equivalent extent. Emission trading is very transparent in terms of its price signal and, while recognising that there are many factors involved in investment and operational decisions, an important issue for the EU is not to lose industry from Europe to other countries (referred to as 'carbon leakage') simply because those other countries might not pursue a similar carbon pricing approach. A multiplicity of actions are, in fact, being taken around the world at various levels of governance, and these actions also have economic impacts, albeit less transparent than an ETS. There is still a perception, however, that free allocation is necessary to alleviate adverse impacts on competitiveness.

The decision was taken in 2005 for there to be free allocation to industry under the EU ETS, and in 2014 the EU's Heads of State and Government decided to continue this approach. This differs from other approaches which some stakeholders proposed, such as putting a carbon price on imports of certain products from third countries by means of making importers subject to the requirement to surrender allowances. The rules for these free allocations are harmonised across the EU, meaning that installations are treated the same whichever Member State they are established in. This is a major step forward in terms of ensuring a level playing field across the EU.

Ahead of the start of phase 3 of the EU ETS in 2013, 52 benchmarks and 3 fall-back approaches for *ex ante* free allocation were agreed with Member States.[8] These EU-wide and fully harmonised benchmarks cover all free allocations taking place under the EU ETS from 2013 onwards (except in respect of modernisation of the power sector as described above). Table 2.1 gives the product benchmarks (based on Annex II to the decision) setting the initial free allocation. In addition to these heat and fuel benchmarks, benchmarks for refineries and aromatic benchmarks are defined.

TABLE 2.1 Product benchmarks for free allocation defined as allowances (tonne CO_2 per 1,000 tonnes produced)

Product	Benchmark	Product	Benchmark	Product	Benchmark
Coke	286	Sintered ore	171	Hot metal	1,328
Pre-bake anode	224	Aluminium	1,514	Grey cement	766
White cement clinker	987	Lime	954	Dolomite	1,072
Sintered dolomite	987	Float glass	453	Bottles & jars colourless	382
Bottles & jars coloured	306	Continuous filament glass fibre	406	Facing bricks	139
Pavers	192	Roof tiles	144	Spray dried powder	76
Plaster	48	Dried secondary gypsum	17	Short fibre kraftpulp	120
Long fibre kraftpulp	60	Sulphite pulp	20	Recovered paper pulp	39

(Continued)

TABLE 2.1 (Continued)

Product	Benchmark	Product	Benchmark	Product	Benchmark
Newsprint	298	Uncoated fine paper	318	Coated fine paper	318
Tissue	334	Testliner and fluting	248	Uncoated carbon board	237
Coated carbon board	273	Nitric acid	302	Adipic acid	2,790
Vinyl chloride monomere	204	Phenol/acetone	266	S-PVC	85
E-PVC	238	Soda ash	843		

The benchmarks take account of the most efficient techniques, substitutes and alternative production processes. All allocations are decided *ex ante* and no free allocation is made in respect of electricity production (except for electricity produced from waste gases, and for the encouragement of modernisation in eight Member States). Free allocation is given to district heating as well as to high-efficiency cogeneration in respect of heating or cooling. Benchmarks are calculated for production, rather than inputs to the production process, to maximise greenhouse gas emission reductions and energy efficiency savings. The starting point for each benchmark was the average performance of the 10% most efficient installations in a sector in the EU in 2005–8 or 2009–10.

The most efficient installations receive allocations around the level of their actual emissions, while less efficient installations are faced with a shortfall. Three quarters of industrial emissions are covered by the 52 product benchmarks. Given the diversity of industrial activities, it is not possible for every product to have a specific benchmark. For the other quarter, there is a hierarchy of approaches. The first is the application of a heat-based energy benchmark (which applies to four fifths of the remaining emissions). The remainder is covered by a fuel-based energy benchmark, or – for a small percentage – is allocated in relation to process emissions based on past emissions levels.

The legislation includes a safeguard clause that ensures that the amount of allowances given out for free through the application of the benchmarks cannot exceed the share of emissions of those installations in the overall EU ETS cap in 2005–7.[9] If this happens, a uniform cross-sectoral correction factor is applied, which operates to reduce allocations uniformly across all beneficiaries of free allocation. In this way, it is ensured that the predetermined limit of free allocation is not exceeded.

The benchmark decision allowed a choice of base years for production values, and this reduced to some extent the stringency of the benchmarks and contributed to the need for the cross-sectoral correction factor to be applied in practice. In 2013, the cross-sectoral correction factor was around 6% increasing to around 18% by 2020. This created some dissatisfaction in industry and led to the realisation that a more refined carbon leakage system may be necessary for the post-2020 period so as to better focus on sectors or sub-sectors where a real competitiveness impact arises.

In recognition of the fact that Europe's cap-and-trade system was not replicated by similar systems in most other major economies in 2009, it was decided that, from 2013 to 2020, allocations to a wide range of industry that are included on a list of those 'deemed to be exposed to carbon leakage' should be at the level of 100% of the benchmarks that are adopted for harmonised free allocation. In the absence of this status, industrial facilities are allocated at 80% of the benchmark in 2013 declining annually and in a linear manner to a level of 30% in 2020. Allocation at a level of 100% of the benchmark still means, however, that a majority of companies are allocated fewer allowances than they are expected to need.

The list of industries 'deemed to be exposed to a significant risk of carbon leakage' was first adopted in 2009[10] for five years, and a new list has been adopted for 2015–19 (see Figure 2.4).[11] While industries cannot be removed from the list during the five-year period, a limited number of additional sectors or subsectors have been added.

A sector is 'deemed to be exposed to a significant risk of carbon leakage' if the sum of additional costs related to both the direct emissions and the indirect impacts from the use of electricity would lead to an increase of production costs of 5% or more and the sector's intensity of trade with third countries is above 10%. Sectors are also included if either EU ETS direct and indirect additional costs would lead to an increase of production costs of at least 30%, or a sector's intensity of trade with third countries exceeds 30%. Most of the sectors and sub-sectors are included on the 2009 list because their intensity of trade with third countries exceeds 30%.[12] The 2009 and 2014 assessments were based on an assumed carbon price of €30 per tonne.

Other sectors have been included on the list based on a qualitative assessment, taking into account the extent to which it is possible for individual installations to reduce emission levels or electricity consumption, current and projected market characteristics, and profit margins.

Based on the harmonised benchmarks, Member States are required to calculate the number of *ex ante* free allowances for each installation, based on EU-wide rules. National implementing measures for all free allocation have been approved by the Commission, and around 6.6 billion allowances are being given out over the period 2013–20.

As concerns new entrants to the EU ETS, 5% of the total quantity of allowances is set aside for new investments, either in terms of entirely new installations or significant capacity extensions of existing installations. Harmonised benchmarking rules are set out for allocations to new entrants. As noted above, a large proportion of the new entrants reserve has been earmarked for specific support for demonstration activities for CCS and innovative renewable energy technologies. With regard to installations that close, the legislation provides that no free allocation is given any longer to an installation that has ceased its operations unless the operator shows that production will be resumed within a reasonable time. The same rule applies for the partial closure of installations or significant reductions of capacity.

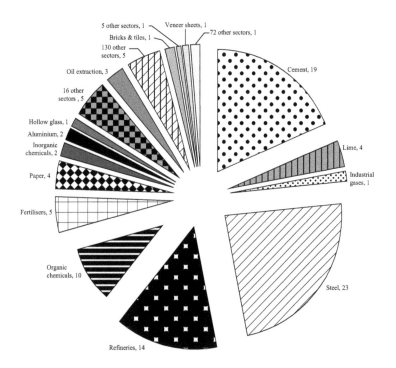

FIGURE 2.4 Share of free allocation (%) based on carbon leakage list, 2015–19

In addition, taking into account the general rule that no free allocation is given to electricity generation, the Directive also states that Member States may grant State aid, i.e. government subsidies, for the benefit of sectors which are found in practice to be exposed to a significant risk of carbon leakage due to emission costs passed on in electricity prices. A number of Member States, including Germany, for example, have granted such State aid, which was approved by the European Commission in 2013.[13]

> Conclusion: of the allowances issued, a little less than half are given out for free to manufacturing industry according to objective criteria, such as technological benchmarks, to shield them from risks of so-called 'carbon leakage'.

The EU ETS covers large stationary emitters

The EU ETS covers more than 11,000 industrial plants, focusing on large stationary emitters, excluding aircraft operators, dealt with in following section. The sectors covered are set out in Annex I to the Directive and include power plants and combustion units larger than 20 MW, oil refineries, iron and steel production, production of non-ferrous metals, cement, lime, pulp and paper, glass, ceramics, bricks, gypsum, mineral wool and ammonia. The coverage was initially limited to CO_2 but, from 2013, emissions of perfluorocarbons from aluminium production and nitrous oxide from adipic acid and nitric acid production in the chemical industry are also covered, extending the coverage of the system by around 100 million tonnes CO_2 equivalent a year.

The EU ETS makes an installation, irrespective of company ownership, subject to ETS coverage if the installed capacity reaches a certain threshold. Alternative concepts like coverage subject to a minimum emissions output or coverage of all installations by a company have not been pursued for reasons of stability in coverage and administration.

Despite this choice, the coverage of combustion units larger than 20 MW required extensive coordination by public authorities across the EU to ensure that the same definition was applied, and the revision of the EU ETS confirmed that 'combustion' means any oxidation of fuels, regardless of the way in which the heat, electrical or mechanical energy produced by this process is used, and any other directly associated activities, including flue gas scrubbing. This clarification is particularly important as regards coverage of the chemicals sector.

While largely harmonised across the EU in terms of coverage, the Directive has specific provisions that allow Member States to vary this scope. First, Member States can individually opt-in other installations and activities. Under these provisions, Member States have included some installations in the EU ETS that would otherwise have fallen under the capacity thresholds. Second, there are provisions for Member States to opt small installations out of the EU ETS. These provisions have been used only by a few Member States to take some smaller installations out of the system, and the opt-out is subject to requirements, such as the introduction of national measures.

> Conclusion: the EU ETS applies to some 11,000 industrial installations in a harmonised way, but Member States may opt-in additional installations.

Extension to emissions from aviation

As of 2012 all flights between European airports are covered by the EU ETS. Coverage of flights from EU airports to third countries, and potential coverage of flights to airports in the EU from third countries, has been postponed until 2017. By that date, agreement on a global market-based mechanism should have been reached in the context of the International Civil Aviation Organization (ICAO). In case of failure, the legislation provides that the original scope will be implemented as of 2017. While aviation comprises less than one tenth of the overall emissions of the EU ETS, it has attracted considerable political attention.

The key features of aviation's inclusion are the following. The legislation[14] applies to all aircraft operators active in the EU market equally. Between 2013 and 2020, the cap was set at 5% below 2004–6 emission levels. 85% of allocations were given out for free based on an efficiency-related benchmark using 2010 levels of activity. Allocations to aircraft operators were based on their respective flight activity in 2010 (measured in terms of the total distance travelled and the total mass of passengers and freight carried). Allocations based on activity reward those that are more efficient.

In terms of scope, the legislation explicitly foresees its amendment to take into account any future agreement adopted at global level, which would clearly be a preferred outcome. Globally, CO_2 emissions from the aviation sector have been growing rapidly and are forecast to continue to increase. By 2020, international aviation emissions are projected to be around 70% higher than 2005 levels. Alongside major modernisation of airspace management, research and development of aviation technology and fuels, market-based measures are an essential part of a comprehensive approach to reduce emissions from aviation.

The ICAO has been very successful in adopting technical standards and operational rules, but States have been reluctant to agree on global economic measures through UN institutions such as the ICAO. In 2004, States in the ICAO concluded that a single global system should not be pursued at the time. Instead, they unanimously agreed to pursue implementation through other avenues, one of which was 'to incorporate emissions from international aviation into Contracting States' emissions trading systems'.[15] This is the avenue that the EU followed.

The EU considers that it is essential for any measure to be non-discriminatory. The US, for example, took the view that permission should be necessary from the US for any US-based airline to be regulated by third countries for any of its activities. The EU Member States have not accepted this claim because of the inevitable market distortions that such an approach would bring if permissions were not forthcoming.

The EU ETS covers the total emissions from a given flight, and is not airspace related. Over-flight of EU territory is not regulated. Several airlines based in the US brought litigation to the highest court in the EU, the European Court of Justice (ECJ), against the EU ETS. In 2011, the Court reached a final judgment that confirmed that the EU ETS law is fully compatible with international law, with the EU/US Open Skies Agreement and the provisions of the Chicago Convention which state that States have the sovereign right to determine the conditions for admission to or departure from their territory and require all airlines to comply. The Court confirmed that the EU's provisions have no extraterritorial effect because no obligations are imposed in the territory of any other State. The requirement to report emissions and to surrender allowances under the EU ETS only arises when an aircraft lands or takes off from an airport in an EU Member State. This point, at which a liability arises, is entirely and exclusively within the EU. The amount of liability depends on the emissions of the flight, taking into account length of journey and specific emissions of the aircraft, but irrespective of whether the flight was to or from another Member State or a third country. This is why the ECJ upheld the measure as not infringing the sovereignty of other States, and not being discriminatory.

Non-discriminatory application of the law is essential. Few business sectors are as international as aviation, and non-discrimination between aircraft operators on flight routes is crucial. Creation of any distortive effect for airlines operating on the same routes in a competitive marketplace must be avoided. The EU has an open aviation market and, for example, commercial flights between the US and Europe are operated not only by EU and US airlines, but also by other airlines, such as Air India and even airlines from Least Developed Countries such as Ethiopian Airways. In addition, US-based carriers like UPS and FedEx operate substantial flights within the EU. Having different treatment for aircraft operators of different nationalities would distort competition between those operating on the same routes, so the EU ETS applies to airlines operating in the European market without distinction as to nationality.

With the inclusion of aviation into the EU ETS, the EU has been ambitious, but has shown clear willingness to adjust its policies in the light of experience. This led to some controversy and future outcomes are not known, but the EU's willingness to lead the way, while respecting international law, is clearly demonstrated. The EU vigorously supports multilateral action in the ICAO to create a global market-based instrument for a sector in which emissions are rising rapidly. But with the 2016 deadline approaching, time is running out very fast to prove that this can be done.

> Conclusion: the scope of the ETS has been extended gradually, also to encompass aviation in Europe. Intensive discussions are ongoing in the context of the ICAO to establish a worldwide market-based instrument to control emissions from international aviation.

The ETS infrastructure

The EU ETS registry: the IT backbone of the carbon market

'Allowances' are the currency of the carbon market and they exist in electronic form. A computerised system to keep track of the ownership of allowances held in electronic accounts is therefore one of the essential requirements for a carbon market to function.

The registry works in much the same way as a bank has a record of all its customers and their money. From 2012 onwards, the 'Union registry' has kept track of all carbon units held in the EU ETS. The registry component has been updated more frequently than any other part of the EU ETS infrastructure, primarily to maintain high standards of security. The registry has no role in trading per se, which is carried out at exchanges that are also involved in trading a range of energy commodities. The Union registry's role is simply to keep a definitive record of the holding of allowances and other units usable in the EU ETS, and of transfers that take place. From a trading perspective, registry transfers is the mechanism by which delivery of allowances from the buyer to the seller takes place.

The EU ETS registry system has been operational since 2005 and has undergone considerable changes. Today it is a centrally managed system that has left behind the more complex set-up that reflected the historical, State-orientated architecture of the Kyoto Protocol (Delbeke, 2006: 1–13). The EU ETS registry based in the European Commission's data centre in Luxembourg has a communication link to the International Transaction Log (ITL) administered by the UNFCCC Secretariat based in Bonn, the main role of which is to issue and transfer Clean Development Mechanism (CDM) and Joint Implementation (JI) credits.

The European Commission and Member States work closely on the operation of the Union registry, with each Member State administrating accounts and, where relevant, providing services in national languages, including helpdesks. Each operator covered by the EU ETS has an account. The second major category of account holders is market intermediaries (banks, brokers) participating in the EU ETS. Individuals can also open accounts.

The registry also facilitates a number of regulatory functions, easing the work of public authorities, market participants and service providers alike. Each year allowances which are handed out for free are transferred into the accounts of operators of installations and airlines by the end of February. Operators report their verified emissions during the previous year by 31 March each year. If this does not take place by then, the registry plays a role in enforcement of rules by public authorities, as transfers out of accounts are automatically blocked.

The Union registry also provides for operators to exchange certain CDM and JI credits, up to certain levels, for EU ETS allowances. Last but not least the information publicly accessible in the registry (verified emissions, surrendered units, etc.) plays an important role for market analysts to provide market participants with robust analysis in order to assure pricing of allowances is based on well-understood facts.

The Union registry also has specific features developed in relation to attempts to undermine, hack into or abuse the system. Transfers of allowances take place within a 26-hour pending period which was one of the security measures introduced following alleged theft of allowances, to limit the speed at which such allowances can be transferred to third parties. Access to the registry is also subject to two-factor authentication, similar to many online banking systems.

Conclusion: the EU ETS registry is a computerised system to keep track of ownership of allowances. Its design and security parameters have evolved in the light of experience and IT developments, as well as through pressures related to cyber security.

Emissions accounting – monitoring, reporting and verification

The rules for monitoring, reporting and verification (MRV) of emissions are, alongside the registries system, another key infrastructure requirement for a carbon market to function properly. Similar to contemporary financial systems underpinned by robust accounting systems, a carbon market needs a solid underpinning by an emissions accounting system. Moreover, the EU ETS installed a system of self-reporting by companies that needs to be verified by an independent third party.

One of the main lessons learned from the EU ETS's pilot phase between 2005 and 2007 is the need for reliable data industry-wide and on plant-specific emissions. There needs to be confidence that emissions are reliably measured and with high accuracy. Given the 'invisible' nature of emissions it is indispensable for operators, buyers and sellers to have trust that a tonne of emissions is really a tonne. This confidence comes from a well-developed set of rules for monitoring, reporting and verification, and activities of competent authorities to check that they are followed in practice.

The first part of these rules is the Regulation for monitoring and reporting of emissions.[16] This Regulation covers the monitoring of direct emissions from stationary installations and from aviation in detail. Emissions are monitored either by measurement using standardised or accepted methods, or on the basis of the calculation using the formula: Activity data × Emission factor × Oxidation factor.[17] A range of default factors have been determined, and the emission factor for biomass is considered to be zero. A separate calculation is made for each activity, installation and for each fuel, and uncertainty levels are also documented. Equally, emissions that are captured and permanently stored are exempted from the surrender requirements, which incentivises the development of CCS technologies.

The second part of the rules is the Regulation on verification and on accreditation of verifiers. Member States are required to ensure that reports submitted by operators are verified by independent third parties by 31 March each year, failing which an operator is not able to make transfers of allowances until a report has been verified as satisfactory. The Regulation for verification and on accreditation of verifiers[18] specifies conditions for the accreditation and withdrawal of accreditation, for mutual recognition and peer evaluation of accreditation bodies.

The verification process addresses the reliability, credibility and accuracy of monitoring systems and the reported data and information relating to emissions, in particular: the reported activity data and related measurements and calculations, the choice and the employment of emission factors, and calculations leading to the determination of the overall emissions. Reported emissions may only be validated if reliable and credible data and information allow the emissions to be determined with a high degree of accuracy, meaning that the reported data is free of inconsistencies, the collection of the data has been carried out in accordance with the applicable scientific standards, and the relevant records of the installation are complete and consistent.

The relative complexity of establishing reliable figures for direct emissions, linked to production, highlights the challenges facing attempts to elaborate detailed estimates of emissions produced from the consumption patterns of countries or specific consumers, as advocated by some. While general patterns can be identified and may be useful in influencing individual consumption decisions and actions, such patterns are far from the level of accuracy that would be needed for using economic instruments to internalise the external costs from greenhouse gas emissions on the basis of consumption. Any border adjustments could only feasibly be applied by using averages and approximations, with the obvious weakness that specific products would be treated unfairly. Averaging to make a consumption-based accounting workable, by definition, would also make it inaccurate.

Conclusion: a well-functioning carbon market requires a solid monitoring and reporting system that sets out clear rules to all market participants.

Developing a robust market oversight regime

Given some unique characteristics of carbon allowances and the lack of prior experience about how carbon markets operate in practice, no tailor-made market oversight rules were included in the initial legal framework. Introducing a stringent market oversight regime from the outset was feared to hamper the development of a carbon price signal based on a liquid market.

As a result of this approach, the EU ETS has rapidly given rise to a liquid market across Europe. While anyone can trade allowances, in practice the most active market participants are power companies with compliance obligations under the EU ETS, and financial intermediaries, who often act on behalf of companies and small emitters.

As detailed above, the carbon market has experienced significant growth in volume and sophistication since 2005. On the basis of experience, regulators have started work to close any gaps in market oversight.

The overwhelming share of EU ETS trading takes place in the 'futures' markets for delivery on a future fixed date, and is therefore covered by pre-existing financial market rules including the Markets in Financial Instruments Directive (MiFID) and the Market Abuse Directive (MAD). These financial rules contain anti-money laundering safeguards (e.g. 'know-your-customer' checks) and, among other things, are intended to ensure that high integrity standards apply to all market participants, prohibiting manipulation through practices such as spreading false information or rumours, and profiting from inside information.

However, a small share (some 5–10% over time) of EU ETS trading has taken place in 'spot' trading markets, for immediate delivery. 'Spot' trading in allowances has lacked consistent regulation at EU level, which made access to the market easy. It is in this area where there have been cases of alleged fraud and theft, with, for a period of time, value added tax (VAT) fraud focusing on carbon markets rather than other traded goods, such as mobile phones and computer chips. The introduction of a system of reverse charging for VAT has largely solved this issue, and the full records of transactions in the registry system have facilitated the follow-up of particular cases by authorities.

The Commission made a proposal in 2011 to revise financial markets rules, including to bring 'spot' trading of allowances under similar regulatory supervision as 'futures' trading. This proposal is being considered by the European Parliament and Council, and should extend the same safeguards to all trading of allowances.

The revised EU ETS legislation gives the specific responsibility to the Commission to monitor the functioning of the European carbon market, and produce an annual report on the functioning of the carbon market, including on the implementation of the auctions, liquidity and the volumes traded. Authority is also conferred on the Commission to act in respect of excessive price fluctuations. In the event that, for more than half a year, the allowance price is more than three times the average price of allowances during the two preceding years, and this does not correspond to changing market fundamentals, auctioning may be brought forward, or up to 25% of the remaining allowances in the new entrants reserve may be auctioned.

EU ETS allowances are entitlements to emit whose legal nature is similar to currency notes rather than to particular possessions. The Registries Regulation has clarified that there is ownership of a particular volume of allowances, rather than rights to specific identifiable allowances, which facilitates judicial consideration of these issues across the EU. In terms of categorisation under international rules, this depends on the area. Allowances are more similar to financial instruments than to goods and services which are covered by the World Trade Organization (WTO), though the trading of allowances is a service which clearly does come under WTO rules.

Conclusion: the EU ETS is already subject to effective market oversight, and the current regime will be further strengthened once the new horizontal financial regulation, related to amendment of the MAD and MiFID, is implemented.

Significant price fluctuations in the EU ETS

During the first 10 years of the ETS, a price signal has been delivered but it has been significantly influenced by the business cycle of economic activity, not least by the worst recession the EU has experienced since the Second World War. On top of that, the EU ETS allowed for the use of international credits created under the Kyoto Protocol, which aggravated significantly the effects of oversupply due to the recession. As the EU ETS has operated in phases, and allowances are created for each phase, the prices per phase are indicated in different shades in Figure 2.5.

In phase 1 (2005–7) the price of EU allowances dropped steeply in the second quarter of 2006 after the first verified emissions figures were reported. It became clear that the Member States had determined an aggregate number of allowances in excess of expected total emissions in 2005 to 2007. Due to the fact that phase 1 allowances could not be banked into phase 2, any excess of allowances would have resulted in a price of zero, as indeed happened for most of 2007. At the same time the market price in 2007 for phase 2 allowances was much higher in view of the market expectation that the system would be much more constrained in the second phase.

A second major price drop came in late 2008–early 2009 as the longer-term effects of the economic and financial crisis became clear. It is important to note that the sectors covered by the EU ETS in aggregate are subject to much stronger swings than the economy overall. Individual sectors covered

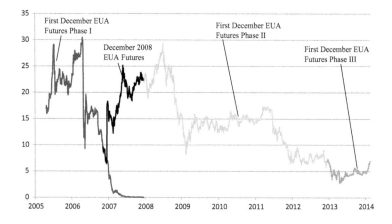

FIGURE 2.5 Market price for European allowances (€/ton)
Source: Bloomberg New Energy Finance.

by the EU ETS saw annual output losses between 2008 and 2009 of over 30%. It was, in fact, largely thanks to the fact that, as of phase 2, allowances could be banked without any restrictions or expiry that the price did not fall further. Together with the design changes agreed in the European Council in 2008, the carbon price stabilised at around €15 for some two years despite deep and prolonged economic recession which gave rise to the emergence of a severe market imbalance.

As of 2009, the supply started to exceed demand so that by the end of phase 2 the market was characterised by a supply overhang of almost 2 billion allowances, which were banked into phase 3 (see Figure 2.6). The growing market imbalance and lack of signs of an economic recovery weighed heavily on the price in 2012 so that it fell to single digits.

The low price of allowances in 2012 gave rise to a debate on what policy action to take to restore market confidence and rejuvenate the European carbon market as a driver for low-carbon investments. The short-term legislative response was to reduce the quantity of allowances for auctioning in 2014 to 2016 by 900 million allowances, and re-inject them into the market in the year 2019–20 when, it was hoped, economic circumstances were more favourable.[19] This proposal, referred to as 'Backloading', was controversial, but nevertheless endorsed by the Council and the European Parliament.

The longer-term legislative response was the proposal, made in early 2014, for a Market Stability Reserve.[20] This proposal provides for allowances to be taken out of the quantities to be auctioned and put into a reserve if the

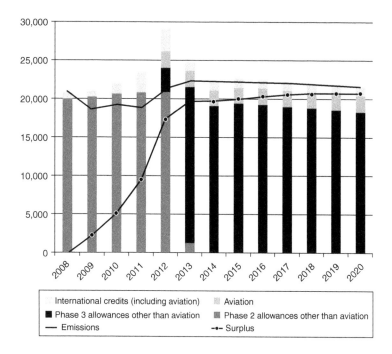

FIGURE 2.6 Surplus of ETS allowances without account taken of the introduction of the Market Stability Reserve

Source: European Commission.

cumulative surplus of allowances in the market exceeded 833 million, and for allowances to be released from the reserve if the cumulative surplus of allowances in the market fell below 400 million allowances.

As such, the Market Stability Reserve was designed to dampen large swings in the supply of allowances on the market in a predictable way. All the rules would be predetermined, so as to minimise discretionary intervention into the market. The purpose was very explicitly to increase the resilience of the EU ETS in the case of pronounced market imbalances emerging.

In May 2015, the Council and the European Parliament reached political agreement on the Market Stability Reserve proposal, including on the date of entry into effect of 1 January 2019, inclusion of backloaded allowances into the reserve, as well as unallocated allowances being transferred directly to the reserve in 2020 and their future usage to be considered under the wider EU ETS review.

There has been active debate around the functioning and design of the EU ETS since its inception. The magnitude of the economic recession from 2008 and continuing slow economic growth were unforeseen. In this context, legislative proposals were made that were considered to be in the best interests of the carbon market. It should be no surprise that it was long debated whether this legislation would not compromise the market's predictability. However, given the unique character of the economic events, regulators intervened, as they did in many other markets, including the saving of financial institutions from collapse.

The Market Stability Reserve, by its predictability, is intended to avoid the need for further market intervention. If the experience of recent years had been known, the EU ETS would without doubt have integrated a Market Stability Reserve mechanism from the outset. Once again, the EU's ability to respond to changed circumstances and learn from experience has been demonstrated.

> Conclusion: the price development in the EU ETS has been subject to considerable fluctuation, mainly as a result of the deep and prolonged economic recession. Decisions have been taken to create a Market Stability Reserve to make the EU ETS more resilient to such economic fluctuation as well as to the influence of other policies that may lead to an unforeseen surplus of allowances.

Pathways to an international carbon market

International credits – linking EU instruments beyond Europe

Apart from establishing a price for greenhouse gas emissions in Europe, the EU ETS has also given incentives for emission reduction projects[21] around the world. This has been through the EU ETS providing the main market for credits from the Kyoto Protocol's two project-based mechanisms, Joint Implementation (JI) and the Clean Development Mechanism (CDM). The biggest demand for CDM credits has in fact come from the EU ETS. By May 2015, the EU ETS has been responsible for the use of approximately 866 million CDM credits (CERs) and 570 million JI credits (ERUs).[22]

The openness of the EU ETS for international credits achieved a number of things. Perhaps the most important one being that constituencies in other countries were made more aware of the opportunities for channelling finance provided by the flexibilities foreseen in the Kyoto Protocol and having involved themselves in reducing emissions locally. This certainly was the case in China. Another benefit of the use of international credits in the ETS is that European businesses had an additional option to meet their obligations by using such credits for compliance purposes, and this increased the overall cost-effectiveness of the system. Despite the fact that the use of external reductions has always been supplemental to domestic reductions within the EU, billions of euros of investments took place through the CDM in sustainable development projects in developing countries including, for example, in renewable energy investments.

The EU relied upon the UNFCCC systems for producing credits in respect of emission reductions, by allowing for the broad use of JI and CDM credits except where emission reductions were either not permanent, as is the case for forestry-based credits, or considered by the EU as politically unacceptable, such as for new nuclear power stations. Apart from these, the EU ETS only set minimum standards for Member States' involvement in approving large hydro-electric projects, and full reliance was placed in the UNFCCC systems for all other issues.

As of 2010, however, the Commission and European Parliament were made aware of serious doubts about the environmental sustainability of credits from projects involving HFC-23 destruction and from adipic acid production in the EU ETS. In 2011, the EU put in place quality standards that would prohibit the use of such JI and CDM credits.[23] With hindsight, this also helped to temper the influx of international credits into an increasingly oversupplied market.

While the EU ETS has been the main market for JI and CDM credits, the relative role of international credits should be kept in perspective. Transactions in the EU ETS have been estimated to make up approximately 84% of the international carbon market activity, while the CDM has made up less than 13% of this activity (out of which a large proportion was to meet demand from operators covered by the EU ETS).

In terms of the EU policy on international credits, the EU ETS has taken a more targeted approach from 2013 onwards. Initially, the EU created a market for CDM projects in China, India and elsewhere as a demonstration of support in the Kyoto system that has not been matched by many other countries. However, such credits do not actually reduce emissions on a global level, but rather displace emissions for reasons of overall economic efficiency. Starting in 2013, the EU ETS therefore restricted credits from new CDM projects only to projects located in States defined by the UN as 'Least Developed Countries' (LDCs). Most of the existing 7,000 CDM projects[24] principally in China, India, Brazil or South Africa, continue to have a market in the EU ETS.

> Conclusion: up to now, the EU ETS has absorbed more than 1.4 billion tonnes of international credits. As of 2013 a more targeted approach is being followed focusing on new CDM projects based in the LDCs.

Linking

In the wake of the 1997 Kyoto Protocol, it was thought by some that an international carbon market could be developed in 'top-down' fashion by the UNFCCC. Article 17 of Kyoto on international emissions trading foresaw that Parties could exchange part of their quantitative commitments. In Kyoto, the US pushed the option of emissions trading very actively, following their success in reducing sulphur emissions inside the US in a cost-effective manner. Moreover, in Kyoto, the US negotiated a target for itself of −7% (compared to 1990) with a view to trading with other Parties who were more generously allocated, such as Russia.

We all know the history. In practice, the US never ratified the Kyoto Protocol, and no one traded with Russia under Article 17. The irony of the story is that international emissions trading was opposed by the EU in the run-up to Kyoto, but since then only the EU has engaged in it. The reason for this is that the EU applies the Kyoto rules of transferring entitlement between EU Member States whenever trading of EU allowances happens between entities located in different Member States. As the EU ETS is about trading between companies, irrespective of where they are located in the EU, there needs to be an automatic and corresponding adjustment in the entitlement of Member States to emit under the Kyoto Protocol. Otherwise, if German power generators, for example, buy allowances in order to emit more, Germany also needs to be entitled to emit more under the Protocol to remain in compliance. These adjustments of Kyoto entitlements happen through the registry without companies even being aware of this matching. This explains, also, why Member States were willing to introduce meaningful and harmonised penalties for companies in non-compliance, as failure by companies would put the country's compliance with its Kyoto Protocol obligations at risk. To this extent, therefore, the EU ETS has been linked, and fully compatible with, the international regime since the outset.

The first formal linking of the EU ETS with other States was the extension to the neighbouring countries of the European Economic Area – Norway, Iceland and Liechtenstein – in 2008, and Croatia has applied the system from 2013 when it joined the EU. Formal linking negotiations are still ongoing with Switzerland.

While the UNFCCC process remains important in a general climate policy context, there has never been a serious attempt to establish a company-based emissions trading system through UN institutions, and it looks unlikely that the international community is sufficiently interested in trying to do so. However, it must be stressed that the existence and continuation of the EU ETS is completely independent of the success or not under the UNFCCC. It should be remembered that the EU ETS started in 2005 prior to the first commitment period of the Kyoto Protocol, although it was built so as to be completely compatible with UN requirements. Its more 'bottom-up' establishment proved useful and important, however, in being able to adapt and correct quickly if needed in the light of experience.

Over the last decade, Europe's share of global greenhouse gas emissions has decreased from around 14% to 9%. Clearly, climate change cannot be addressed effectively without broader action by other countries. Action is increasingly being taken through national initiatives. For various reasons, including the generally positive experience with the EU ETS, other developed and developing countries are establishing their own emissions trading systems. There is a growing recognition that the magnitude of the climate change challenge requires that a price be put on greenhouse gas emissions in order for market forces to be effectively harnessed to deliver the necessary emission reductions. Without effective pricing approaches, companies will not have the incentives or economic interest to invest in low-carbon activities.

Legislation to put a price on emissions will be passed by national legislatures, whether in the form of emissions trading or taxes on emissions, such as Ireland put in place for emissions outside the scope of the EU ETS. The difficulty of putting such legislation in place was demonstrated by the US's inability to pass Federal legislation to put a price on emissions since the McCain–Lieberman bill that was first proposed in 2003. At Federal level, the US came close to having a similar system to the EU ETS, by the House of Representatives' passage of the Waxman–Markey bill in 2009. However, the companion bill in the Senate, the Kerry–Boxer bill (S. 1733), was not passed and the near-term prospects for passage of legislation in the US Congress that puts a price on greenhouse gas emissions appear low.

Other regions of the world have also been developing market-based measures to tackle climate change. Australia, after difficult domestic discussions, established a national emissions trading system that initially functioned as a tax and would have moved to being an emissions trading system. It was foreseen to be linked with the EU ETS. However, the current government halted further development of this approach.

The most promising policy experiments are today happening in Asia. South Korea has a national greenhouse gas emissions trading system that is up and running as of January 2015. China has established seven pilot emissions trading systems, covering some 15–20% of the economy and plans are on the table to extend these towards a nationwide system.[25] California has an emissions trading system operating since January 2013. New Zealand also has an emissions trading system that has been in operation since 2008, and the North-Eastern States in the US have been operating the Regional Greenhouse Gas Initiative, RGGI, since 2009.[26]

It is widely underestimated how much the emergence of these national and sub-national emissions trading systems also offer the prospect for the development of an international carbon market. Indeed carbon allowances can be traded across jurisdictions and a common carbon price can be established within a geographically wider area over time. This process is enabled by a provision in the legal framework of the EU ETS which allows for 'linking' of carbon markets by means of mutual recognition of carbon allowances. The procedural step needed is a bilateral agreement between the EU and a third country.

The 'bottom-up' development of an international carbon market via national legislation, and linking agreements between them, will take time. In order to facilitate such a process, bilateral cooperation as well as programmes, such as the World Bank's Partnership for Market Readiness, has proved to be very valuable. The potential for more cost-effectiveness is clearly there, but linking systems first needs robust and environmentally effective cap-and-trade systems to be put in place. Only then will an international market be achieved.

> Conclusion: the EU is open to engage in linking its ETS to other comparable systems so as to create over time a global carbon price through a truly international market. It believes such an international market will best be achieved through a bottom-up process rather than through top-down approaches overseen by the UN.

Notes

1 Article 1(9) of Directive 2009/29/EC of the European Parliament and of the Council of 23 April 2009 amending Directive 2003/87/EC so as to improve and extend the greenhouse gas emission allowance trading scheme of the Community; OJ L 140, 5.6.2009, pp. 63–87: http://eur-lex.europa.eu/legal-content/EN/TXT/PDF/?uri=CELEX:32009L0029&from=EN

2 The year 2005 is used as the reference year for ETS sectors because this is the first year for which comparable monitoring, reporting and verification data are available for all installations covered by the system.

3 More details of about this Fund, and the investments it has contributed to, can be obtained from the website of the European Commission at: http://ec.europa.eu/clima/policies/lowcarbon/ner300/index_en.htm

4 Article 1(12) (inserting new Article 10c) of Directive 2009/29/EC of the European Parliament and of the Council of 23 April 2009 amending Directive 2003/87/EC so as to improve and extend the greenhouse gas emission allowance trading scheme of the Community; OJ L 140, 5.6.2009, pp. 63–87: http://eur-lex.europa.eu/legal-content/EN/TXT/PDF/?uri=CELEX:32009L0029&from=EN

5 See Council of European Union document date 12.12.2008 (Reference: 17215/08) 'Energy and climate change – Elements of the final compromise': 'The European Council recalls that Member States will determine, in accordance with their respective constitutional and budgetary requirements, the use of revenues generated from the auctioning of allowances in the EU emissions trading system. It takes note of their willingness to use at least half of this amount for actions to reduce greenhouse gas emissions, mitigate and adapt to climate change, for measures to avoid deforestation, to develop renewable energies, energy efficiency as well as other technologies contributing to the transition to a safe and sustainable low-carbon economy, including through capacity building, technology transfers, research and development': www.consilium.europa.eu/uedocs/cms_data/docs/pressdata/en/ec/104672.pdf

6 European Commission (2014) Progress towards achieving the Kyoto and EU 2020 objectives, Brussels (COM(2014) 689 final dated 28 October 2014): http://ec.europa.eu/transparency/regdoc/rep/1/2014/EN/1-2014-689-EN-F1-1.Pdf; see page 14 of report.

7 Article 1(12) (inserting new Article 10(2) and new Annexes IIa & IIb) of Directive 2009/29/EC of the European Parliament and of the Council of 23 April 2009 amending Directive 2003/87/EC so as to improve and extend the greenhouse gas emission allowance trading scheme of the Community; OJ L 140, 5.6.2009, pp. 63–87: http://eur-lex.europa.eu/legal-content/EN/TXT/PDF/?uri=CELEX:32009L0029&from=EN

8 Commission Decision 2011/278/EU of 27 April 2011 determining transitional Union-wide rules for harmonised free allocation of emission allowances pursuant to Article 10a of Directive 2003/87/EC of the European Parliament and of the Council; OJ L 130, 17.5.2011, pp. 1–45: http://eur-lex.europa.eu/legal-content/EN/TXT/PDF/?uri=CELEX:32011D0278&from=EN

9 Article 1(12) (inserting new Article 10a(5)) of Directive 2009/29/EC of the European Parliament and of the Council of 23 April 2009 amending Directive 2003/87/EC so as to improve and extend the greenhouse gas emission allowance trading scheme of the Community; OJ L 140, 5.6.2009, pp. 63–87: http://eur-lex.europa.eu/legal-content/EN/TXT/PDF/?uri=CELEX:32009L0029&from=EN

10 Commission Decision 2011/278/EU of 24 December 2009 determining, pursuant to Directive 2003/87/EC of the European Parliament and of the Council, a list of sectors and subsectors which are deemed to be exposed to a significant risk of carbon leakage; OJ L 1, 5.1.2010, pp. 10–18: http://eur-lex.europa.eu/legal-content/EN/TXT/PDF/?uri=CELEX:32010D0002&from=EN. This decision was subsequently amended in 2011, 2012 and 2013; for more details see: http://ec.europa.eu/clima/policies/ets/cap/leakage/documentation_en.htm

11 Commission Decision 2014/746/EU of 27 October 2014 determining, pursuant to Directive 2003/87/EC of the European Parliament and of the Council, a list of sectors and subsectors which are deemed to be exposed to a significant risk of carbon leakage, for the period 2015 to 2019 (notified under document C(2014) 7809); OJ L 308, 29.10.2014, pp. 114–24: http://eur-lex.europa.eu/legal-content/EN/TXT/PDF/?uri=CELEX:32014D0746&from=EN

12 The level of disaggregation for sectors and sub-sectors was undertaken at a detailed level, so-called 'NACE-4', with more disaggregated analysis for specific sub-sectors where this was considered justified.

13 Currently, Belgium (Flanders), Germany, Greece, the Netherlands, Norway, Spain and the UK are compensating for indirect costs. State aid reference for Germany: SA.36103 State aid for indirect CO_2 costs (ETS).

14 Directive 2008/101/EC of the European Parliament and of the Council of 19 November 2008 amending Directive 2003/87/EC so as to include aviation activities in the scheme for greenhouse gas emission allowance trading within the Community; OJ L 8, 13.1.2009, pp. 3–21.

15 Assembly Resolutions in Force, Doc. 9848, Published by authority of the Secretary General, International Civil Aviation Organization (as of 8 October 2004): www.icao.int/environmental-protection/Documents/a35–5.pdf

16 Commission Regulation (EU) No. 601/2012 of 21 June 2012 on the monitoring and reporting of greenhouse gas emissions pursuant to Directive 2003/87/EC of the European Parliament and of the Council; OJ L 181, 12.7.2012, pp. 30–104: http://eur-lex.europa.eu/legal-content/EN/TXT/PDF/?uri=CELEX:32012R0601&from=EN

17 An example for an activity is the combustion of coal, an example for an emissions factor is the emissions per unit of coal combusted; the oxidation factor is a technical feature to account for the incomplete combustion of coal as a result of which not all emissions are released into the atmosphere.

18 Commission Regulation (EU) No. 600/2012 of 21 June 2012 on the verification of greenhouse gas emission reports and tonne-kilometre reports and the accreditation of verifiers pursuant to Directive 2003/87/EC of the European Parliament and of the Council; OJ L 181, 12.7.2012, pp. 1–29.

19 Commission Regulation (EU) No. 176/2014 of 25 February 2014 amending Regulation (EU) No. 1031/2010 in particular to determine the volumes of greenhouse gas emission allowances to be auctioned in 2013–20; OJ L 56, 26.2.2014, pp. 11–13: http://eur-lex.europa.eu/legal-content/EN/TXT/PDF/?uri=CELEX:32014R0176&from=EN

20 Proposal for a Decision of the European Parliament and of the Council concerning the establishment and operation of a market stability reserve for the Union greenhouse gas emission trading scheme and amending Directive 2003/87/EC of 22.1.2014: http://eur-lex.europa.eu/legal-content/EN/TXT/PDF/?uri=CELEX:52014PC0020&from=EN

21 Although it is important to keep in mind that the credits of these emission reductions outside Europe give rise to a corresponding increase in emissions within the EU. This feature has been frequently misunderstood.

22 European Commission Press Release, Brussels, 16 May 2013: 'Emissions trading: 2012 saw continuing decline in emissions but growing surplus of allowances': http://www.europa.eu/rapid/press-release_IP-13–437_en.doc and European Commission Regulatory Update of 4 May 2015 at: http://ec.europa.eu/clima/news/articles/news_2015050402_en.htm

23 Commission Regulation (EU) No. 550/2011 of 7 June 2011 on determining, pursuant to Directive 2003/87/EC of the European Parliament and of the Council, certain restrictions applicable to the use of international credits from projects involving industrial gases; OJ L 149, 8.6.2011, pp. 1–3: http://eur-lex.europa.eu/legal-content/EN/TXT/PDF/?uri=CELEX:32011R0550&from=EN

24 UNFCCC News Release: Kyoto Protocol's clean development mechanism reaches milestone at 7,000 registered projects: https://cdm.unfccc.int/CDMNews/issues/issues/I_8XM9FF99N0WN7MMK9XFBJLSX23LX8Q/viewnewsitem.html

25 Han, G., Olsson, M., Hallding, K., and Lunsford, D. (2012) 'China's Carbon Emission Trading: An Overview of Current Development', FORES, Bellmansgatan 10, SE-118 20 Stockholm: www.sei-international.org/mediamanager/documents/Publications/china-cluster/SEI-FORES-2012-China-Carbon-Emissions.pdf

26 ICAP, 2015: Emissions Trading Worldwide: ICAP Status Report 2015: https://icapcarbonaction.com/images/StatusReport2015/ICAP_Report_2015_02_10_online_version.pdf

References

Alexeeva-Talebi, V. (2010) *Cost Pass-Through of the EU Emissions Allowances: Examining the European Petroleum Markets* Discussion Paper No. 10-086, ZEW, Mannheim (ftp://ftp.zew.de/pub/zew-docs/dp/dp10086.pdf, consulted 31 March 2014).

Delbeke, J. (2006) (ed.) *EU Environmental Law: The EU Greenhouse Gas Emissions Trading Scheme.* Claeys & Casteels, Leuven.

Ellerman, A.D., and Buchner, B. (2008) Over-Allocation or Abatement? A Preliminary Analysis of the EU ETS Based on the 2005–06 Emissions Data. *Environmental and Resource Economics* 41(2) 267–287. (http://link.springer.com/article/10.1007%2Fs10640-008-9191-2#).

Ellerman, A.D., Convery, F.J., and de Perthuis, C. (2010) *The European Union Emission Trading Scheme*, Cambridge University Press, Cambridge.

Lise, W., Sijm, J., and Hobbs, B.F. (2010) 'The Impact of the EU ETS on Prices, Profits and Emissions in the Power Sector: Simulation Results with the COMPETES EU20 Model'. *Environmental and Resource Economics* (47) 23–44.

Sijm, J., Hers, S., Lise, W., and Wetzelaer, B. (2008) 'The Impact of the EU ETS on Electricity Prices', ECN, Petten, ECN-E-08–007, December 2008 (http://re.indiaenvironmentportal.org.in/files/e08007.pdf, consulted 31 March 2014).

Solier, B., and Jouvet, P.A. (2013) 'An Overview of CO_2 Cost Pass-through to Electricity Prices in Europe'. *Energy Policy* (61) 1370–1376.

3
CLIMATE-RELATED ENERGY POLICIES

Jos Delbeke, Ger Klaassen and Stefaan Vergote

The EU's energy policy: towards a more sustainable, more secure and more competitive energy system

Unlike environmental issues, the EU Treaty incorporated the field of energy policy only recently. Only from 2009 did the so-called Lisbon Treaty (the Treaty on the Functioning of the European Union) include specific provisions relating to energy policy. In its Article 194 it is specified that the EU's energy policy shall aim, in a spirit of solidarity between Member States, to:

1 ensure the functioning of the energy market;
2 ensure security of energy supply in the Union;
3 promote energy efficiency and energy saving and the development of new and renewable forms of energy; and
4 promote the interconnection of energy networks.

All this should be done taking account of the need to preserve and improve the environment and in the context of the establishment and functioning of the internal market. In terms of procedure, the European Parliament and the Council, acting in accordance with the ordinary legislative procedure (or 'co-decision', as it was previously known), shall establish the measures necessary to achieve the above objectives.

In contrast to environmental policy, many energy issues are still decided at national level. This is most evident for issues related to the energy mix. Even now under the Lisbon Treaty, it is explicitly stated that the EU's energy policy shall neither affect a Member State's right to determine the conditions for exploiting its energy resources, nor its choice between different energy sources and the general structure of its energy supply.

Procedures aside, the current way of consuming and producing energy in the EU is, at the moment, neither sustainable, nor secure, nor competitive. First, current levels of energy use contribute significantly (around 80% in the EU) to greenhouse gas emissions both in the EU and globally. Energy use also affects air pollution, water pollution and land use.

Second, the security of energy supply in the EU is at risk. In 2012 the EU-28's overall dependency on energy imports was 53% (compared with 43% in 1995). In 2012 the EU imported 86% of its oil compared to 74% in 1995. Gas imports increased to 66% in 2012 up from 43% in 1995.[1] More importantly, the imports do not always come from politically stable regions and, most notably, gas comes from a limited number of countries. In 2013, 67% of the EU oil imports came from only five countries: Russia, Norway, Saudi Arabia, Nigeria and Iran. In the same year 87% of natural gas imports were supplied by just five countries: Russia, Norway, Algeria, Qatar and Nigeria. During the last decade, gas supply to the EU was disrupted in 2006, 2008 and 2009.[2] More recently, the crisis between Ukraine and Russia has raised the question of possible interruptions in the supply of gas from Russia. The IEA (2012) has forecasted that, on the basis of current policies, the EU's import dependency for oil and gas (calculated as net imports divided by primary energy demand for each fuel) will increase through to 2035 (see Figure 3.1).

Third, another issue of concern is the impact of energy costs on the competiveness of European industry in relation to its main competitors. This issue became more prominent as a result of the rapid development of shale gas in the US. This led to a divergence of gas wholesale prices between the US and the EU, reaching a factor 3 to 4 times higher gas prices in Europe in the period 2011–2012. This led to fears that new investment in, for example, the petro-chemical or gas-intensive industries, would move outside the EU. However, since then, the divergence has decreased to a factor of two.

Important progress has been made in the field of the internal market. Consecutive legislative packages have forced the unbundling of traditionally vertically integrated energy companies. Over the years, liquid wholesale markets have been established in electricity and gas. Nevertheless, the creation

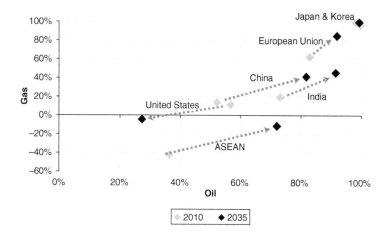

FIGURE 3.1 Net oil and gas import dependency by region
Source: © OECD/IEA 2012 *World Energy Outlook,* IEA Publishing.

of a truly integrated EU internal market for electricity and gas is far from complete:

1   Interconnections are still insufficient in many areas to allow for cross-border trade and competition, and connect 'energy islands' such as the Baltic States or the Iberian peninsula to the rest of the EU.
2   Regulated tariffs, market dominance by incumbents, and low switching rates are evidence of too low levels of competition in retail markets.
3   Public intervention at national level has been steadily increasing, notably in the field of renewable energy and capacity mechanisms, leading to increasing concerns of fragmentation of the internal market and distortions of competition.

One of the major developments – and achievements – of the past 10 years has been the alignment and coordination of energy and climate policies. This arises from the strategic view that, for a region such as the EU that is largely dependent on imports of fossil fuels, the instruments and technologies to achieve a more competitive and secure energy system largely coincide with those needed to reduce greenhouse gas emissions, notably:

1   increasing energy efficiency;
2   increased utilisation of low-carbon technologies, such as renewables, nuclear, and, in the future, potentially coal combined with Carbon Capture and Storage;

3   accelerating innovation in low-carbon and energy efficient technologies as a means to create a competitive edge in rapidly growing global markets for these products, and one of the means to ensure long-term sustainable growth (see also Stiglitz, 2013).

In this context, it is important to highlight the compatibility and complementarity of the EU ETS with the functioning of electricity markets. The EU ETS needs a well-functioning electricity market so that competition in dispatch and investment enables a shift to low-carbon generation. Integrating the price of CO_2 fully in the price-setting mechanisms of a liberalised electricity market, rather than replacing it 'outside the market' through specific interventions, will ensure that emissions are being reduced where it is cheapest to do so.

The purpose of this chapter is to describe the major EU energy policy instruments that try to address the above problems. However, their examination is confined to how they relate to climate policy and the need to reduce greenhouse gas emissions. This means, in particular, that this chapter does neither deal with issues related to the development of a single European energy market nor with measures that are specifically addressed to increase energy supply security.

Energy policy in the EU is evolving fast, and in February 2015, the Commission outlined a strategy towards the establishment of a 'resilient Energy Union with a forward looking climate policy'.[3] The strategy is being built around five dimensions:

1   energy security, solidarity and trust;
2   a fully integrated European energy market;
3   energy efficiency contributing to moderation of demand;
4   decarbonising the economy; and
5   research, innovation and competitiveness.

What is more, the Energy Union strategy is accompanied by an ambitious plan of action entailing 15 concrete action points. The approach confirms the strategic alignment of the climate and energy agenda. Important further developments can be expected in the coming years, building on and learning from the policies described in this chapter.

This chapter has the following structure: the second section deals with renewable energy. The third section deals with energy efficiency; the fourth section covers the regulations related to the emissions of passenger cars, vans, lorries and ships and the final section looks ahead.

Renewable Energy

The Renewable Energy Sources Directive

The Renewable Energy Sources Directive was agreed in its present form as part of the climate and energy package adopted early in 2009.[4] The Directive aims to increase the share of renewable energy in the EU to 20% of gross final energy consumption in the year 2020. Renewable energy covers wind energy, solar energy (for heat and electricity), hydropower, tidal and wave power, geothermal energy and biomass energy. Extra energy generated through heat pumps and renewable electricity used in transport also counts towards the renewable energy target.

Renewable energy provides an essential alternative to energy from (mostly imported) fossil fuels. Increasing its contribution is expected to reduce greenhouse gas emissions, increase energy supply security and promote innovation and technological development while at the same time providing employment opportunities. In 2005 the share of renewable energy in the EU was 8.5%. In 2013 the share had increased to approximately 15% (see Table 3.1).

To achieve the overall objective of a 20% share in 2020, legally binding objectives for the share of renewable energy in national energy consumption were agreed for each Member State. Such mandatory targets were expected to provide the business sector with the long-term stability needed to make investments in renewables. It was left to each Member State to meet its national target through national policy measures.

The starting point for defining the quantitative target for each Member State was the share of renewable energy in its energy mix in 2005. The overall renewable energy share was 8.5% in 2005, so an additional 11.5% needed to be found. Consequently, a flat-rate additional percentage was allocated uniformly to all Member States (5.75%), and a further equivalent effort was distributed on the basis of GDP *per capita*. Finally, a small adjustment was made for the five Member States who had taken most early action.

Table 3.1 shows the mandatory objectives of all EU countries as well as the progress made up to 2013. By June 2010, each Member State was required to submit a National Renewable Energy Action Plan to the European Commission. This Plan had to specify, among other things, the energy consumption of the Member State, the targets per sector (electricity, heating and cooling, and transport) and the national measures that were expected to be taken to reach these targets.

Every single Member State developed its own national support schemes, and as a result a wide variety emerged. This implied that Member States in principle had control over the costs of their own schemes. However, when the unit costs of renewables started to tumble, Member States were generally slow to adapt their support schemes, and this created situations of overly generous subsidies. This undermined the credibility of the policy, which coincided with the budgetary crisis that spread over Europe. As a result the support schemes were modified and sometimes even subject to retroactive revisions.

The Renewables Directive also foresees some flexibility allowing Member States to reach part of the target outside their territory. The Commission was much more outspoken on the need for such flexibilities, notably through harmonised 'guarantees of origin' that would facilitate cross-border trade, in an attempt to reach the overall target cost-effectively.[5] Many Member States, however, feared that such a system would undermine their freedom to determine their own support schemes. In addition they were reluctant to pay for renewable energy investments in other Member States, while leaving the co-benefits, such as in terms of energy security and 'green jobs', in the country where the investment takes place. Similarly, the renewable energy sector feared that successful support schemes would be undermined.

Therefore, during the interinstitutional decision-making process, only weak flexibility provisions were adopted. First, the Directive provided that physical consumption of renewable energy in a Member State other than the one it was produced in could be taken into account (such as the export of hydroelectricity from Austria to Germany). Second, the Directive also allowed that renewable energy paid for and consumed (but not physically transferred) in one Member State could count towards the national target of another Member State. This would have to be subject to the agreement of both Member States concerned. These 'cooperation mechanisms' included either joint projects between Member States (such as the building of a large-scale solar plant), or joint support schemes or statistical transfers (see Articles 6–10 of the Directive). Significantly, however, these flexibilities had to be agreed between the Member States themselves, and not only between operators.

Progress towards 2020 renewable energy targets

Table 3.1 indicates that the vast majority of Member States (as well as the EU as a whole) made good progress and met their interim renewable energy targets for 2011/2012).[6] Total use of renewable energy in 2011 dropped compared to 2010 but the latest data (from March 2015) show that the share of renewables in gross inland consumption of energy increased to 15% in 2013.[7]

The increase in the use of renewable energy by type of renewable in the EU since 1990 has been impressive, as can be seen from Figure 3.2

TABLE 3.1 Progress towards national renewable energy targets for 2020

	2005	2011	2012	Target 2011/2012	2013	Objective 2020
EU-28	8.7	12.9	14.1	10.7	15.0	20.0
Belgium	2.3	5.2	6.8	4.4	7.9	13.0
Bulgaria	9.5	14.6	16.3	10.7	19.0	16.0
Czech Republic	6.0	9.3	11.2	7.5	12.4	13,0
Denmark	15.6	24.0	26.0	19.6	27.2	30.0
Germany	6.7	11.6	12.4	8.2	12.4	18.0
Estonia	17.5	25.6	25.8	10.7	25.6	25.0
Ireland	2.8	6.6	7.2	5.7	7.8	13.0
Greece	7.0	10.9	13.8	9.1	15.0	18.0
Spain	8.5	13.2	14.3	10.9	15.4	20.0
France	9.5	11.3	13.4	10.7	14.2	20.0
Croatia	12.8	15.4	16.8	No target	18.0	20.0
Italy	5.9	12.3	13.5	7.6	16.7	17.0
Cyprus	3.1	6.0	6.8	0.9	8.1	13,0
Latvia	32.3	33.5	35.8	34.0	37.1	42.0
Lithuania	17.0	20.2	21.7	16.6	23.0	23.0
Luxembourg	1.4	2.9	3.1	2.9	3.6★	11.0
Hungary	4.5	9.1	9.6	6.0	9.8	13.0
Malta	0.3	0.7	2.7	2.0	3.8	10.0
Netherlands	2.3	4.3	4.5	4.7	4.5	14.0
Austria	24.0	30.8	32.1	25.4	32.6	34.0
Poland	7.0	10.4	11.0	8.8	11.3	15.0
Portugal	19.5	24.5	24.6	22.6	25.7	31.0
Romania	17.6	21.2	22.9	19.0	23.9	24.0
Slovenia	16.0	19.4	20.2	17.8	21.5	25.0
Slovakia	5.5	10.3	10.4	8.2	9.8	14.0
Finland	28.9	32.7	34.3	30.4	36.8	38.0
Sweden	40.5	48.8	51.0	41.6	52.1	49.0
United Kingdom	1.4	3.8	4.2	4.0	5.1	15.0

Source: Eurostat; estimates based on the national data transmission under Regulation (EC) No. 1099/2008 on energy statistics.

Note: ★ is an estimate by Eurostat.

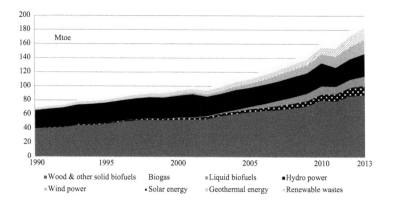

FIGURE 3.2 The development of renewable energy use in the EU by type of renewable
Source: Eurostat.

(Eurostat, 2014).[8] There has been a steady increase across all types of renewables, most notably in wind and solar. Also wood, biogas and liquid biofuels show remarkable growth.

Falling costs and rapid globalisation of the renewable energy industry

The costs of producing electricity using renewable energy (for example, solar photovoltaic (PV) but also wind energy and some biomass technologies) have been reduced considerably over the past years. Figure 3.3 shows that the average costs (in €/MWh) of electricity generated by onshore wind turbines in Denmark and Germany dropped significantly over time as a result of learning-by-doing (based on Klaassen et al., 2005). Each time capacity doubled investment per kilowatt capacity dropped by 8% to 11%, starting from an initial level of around €2,000/kW. At a global level similar cost reductions have been observed.[9] Similarly costs of PV modules (in €/W) have fallen by over 80% since 2009. The costs of installed rooftop PV systems fell by 65% between 2006 and 2012 in Germany enabling solar PV to undercut residential electricity tariffs. The costs are expected to continue to fall over time, and this is the most striking for capital costs. For solar PV modules costs might still be reduced by up to 22% in the future for every doubling of capacity (JRC, 2014a).[10] For offshore wind, capital costs could drop by 7% each time capacity doubles. By 2030 this would reduce investment costs by some 25–27% for offshore wind and commercial solar PV. For onshore wind, cost reductions are typically lower, but this technology has come to a point of being nearly competitive with conventional power plants.

These cost reductions have been accompanied by rapid globalisation. This has led to first-mover advantages, in particular for companies and countries that were able to benefit from a stable local demand. In the wind sector, those countries that were the first to develop a strong demand-side policy, such as Denmark, Spain and Germany, are still home to some of the world's leading companies in this field. However, evidence shows that the first-mover advantages should not be taken for granted. This is particularly true in the PV sector. European and Japanese companies went through a strong demand-driven growth, but now face tough competition by, most notably, Chinese companies that have now the biggest market shares globally (Pollit et al., 2015: 14).

The evolution of cost reduction has been accompanied by rapid globalisation, but also by replication of similar renewable energy policies across the globe. Today, China is not only the largest producer of wind and solar components, but also the largest installer.

Fuels and biofuels

The Renewable Energy Sources Directive also requires that at least 10% of all energy used in the transport sector comes from renewable sources in 2020. This mainly involves biofuels (liquid or gaseous fuels made from

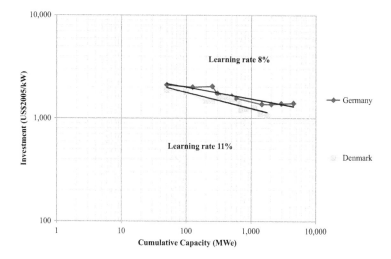

FIGURE 3.3 Renewables policies contribute to reducing technology cost

biomass), such as ethanol and biodiesel, but also includes the use of electricity from renewable sources in the transport sector (for example, for trains). This 10% objective is to be met by each EU Member State in 2020. This sub-target (as it contributes also to the 20% renewable energy target) is the same for each country, as transport fuels are easily traded and transported within the EU.

In parallel, since 2009, Article 7a(2) of the Fuel Quality Directive[11] requires a reduction of the greenhouse gas intensity of fuels used in vehicles by up to 6% by 2020. The Fuel Quality Directive has existed for several decades, and addresses air pollution caused by the use of road fuels through regulating, for example, lead and sulphur content of fuels. Common fuel quality rules are important as they not only ensure that there can be a single market for road transport fuels, but also that vehicles can be driven safely, without causing damage to engines, using fuels bought anywhere in the EU in the course of a journey.

The Fuel Quality Directive establishes an obligation on suppliers of transport fuels. Suppliers can choose to act as a group to jointly meet the targets. Calculation of the greenhouse gas intensity of fuels is based on a life-cycle analysis. This means that all emissions from the extraction, processing and distribution of fuels are included, wherever possible. Hence, a 'well-to-wheels' approach is required. Direct life-cycle greenhouse gas emission reductions are calculated from a 2010 baseline of fossil fuel greenhouse gas intensity.

For biofuels to count towards the greenhouse gas emission reduction targets of the Fuel Quality Directive, as well as the provisions of the Renewable Energy Sources Directive, certain sustainability criteria must be achieved. These should minimise the undesirable impacts of their production. The criteria require that greenhouse gas emissions must be at least 35% lower than from the fossil fuels they replace. From 2017 this increases to 50%, and from 2018 the savings must be at least 60% for new installations.

Biofuels and bioliquids shall not be made from raw material derived from land with a high biodiversity value (e.g. primary forest), a high carbon stock (e.g. wetlands) or land that was peat land. However, more often the pressure to convert land does not come from the wish to produce biofuels directly on the converted land, but rather to produce food that would otherwise have been produced on existing agricultural land now used to produce biofuels. This 'knock-on' effect is called 'Indirect Land-Use Change' (ILUC).

ILUC may significantly reduce the greenhouse gas savings from biofuels, and if it is not taken into account, the environmental added-value of using biofuels in the first place can be greatly exaggerated (and even eliminated altogether). Furthermore, and rather more obviously, the use of biofuels can also conflict with food production: often the same raw materials can be used to produce both food and biofuels. So-called 'first-generation' biofuels are usually produced from cereal crops (e.g. wheat, maize), oil crops (e.g. rapeseed, palm oil) and sugar crops (e.g. sugar beet, sugar cane) using established technology. However, 'second-generation' or 'advanced' biofuels usually use non-food feedstock, such as straw and waste, or algae and non-food crops grown on land that would not otherwise be used for food or feed production (e.g. miscanthus and short-rotation coppice).

For these reasons, the European Commission proposed an amendment to the Fuel Quality Directive as well as to the Renewable Energy Sources Directive to limit the amount of food-based biofuels to 5%, which was approximately equal to the current (2012) consumption level at that time. This constraint is expected to allow non-food-based biofuels to make a greater contribution to meeting the 10% renewable energy in transport target. At the same time, second-generation and advanced biofuels would be promoted as they are expected to have low or no indirect land use emissions associated with them. In April 2015 agreement was reached between the European Parliament and Council on the ILUC proposal including a percentage cap on food-based first-generation biofuels of 7%.

After a promising start, the target of a 10% share renewable energy in transport fuels may not be met.[12] In 2010 the share was only 4.7% while the planned share was 4.9%, the bulk of which was biodiesel, followed by bio-gasoline.[13] In 2013 the share was 5.3%.[14] Progress made in implementing the biofuel sustainability criteria is clearly not sufficient in the absence of provisions that adequately address ILUC. Furthermore, regarding the risk of biodiversity loss related to the domestic and imported biofuels, although it has been found that production from most EU countries poses a low risk for biodiversity losses, biofuel imports from Brazil (soy and sugar), the US (soy and maize) and Russia (rapeseed and soy), on the other hand, were assessed to be at high risk of causing biodiversity loss.[15]

The experience with the EU's regulation on fuels and biofuels has not always provided sufficient regulatory certainty for businesses, but also the scientific evidence still raises doubts about the environmental added-value of biofuels and bioliquids. The European Commission indicated that for these reasons it does not intend to propose new targets for renewable energy or for the greenhouse gas intensity of fuels in the transport sector beyond 2020.[16] The European Council's Conclusions of October 2014 did not contradict such a change of approach, but invited the Commission 'to further examine instruments and measures for a comprehensive and technology neutral approach for the promotion of emissions reductions and energy efficiency in transport, for electric transportation and for renewable energy sources in transport also after 2020'.

Opportunities and challenges: cost-effectiveness and market integration

Excessive divergence between the support schemes of the Member States, the limited use of the cooperation mechanisms, and the pressure on available public money following the economic recession, necessitated the European Commission to define a more orderly framework for the delivery of renewable targets.

In 2013, the Commission encouraged Member States to develop more cost-effective schemes adaptable over time to technological progress, so as to keep costs in check.[17] It was also stressed that specific barriers hindering the diffusion of renewable energy (administrative burdens, slow infrastructure build and delays in connections, as well as grid operating rules that disadvantage renewable energy) were not always adequately removed.

In 2014, new guidelines on State aid for projects in the field of environmental protection and energy were adopted.[18] These guidelines contained the following key elements:

1   To promote a gradual move to market-based support for renewable energy by 2017. Some renewable energy technologies are already mature, which calls for their integration in the market. To increase cost-effectiveness and limit distortions, the new guidelines foresee the gradual introduction of competitive bidding processes for allocating public support, while offering flexibility to take account of national circumstances. The guidelines also foresee the gradual replacement of feed-in tariffs by feed-in premiums, which increase the exposure of renewable energy to market price signals.
2   To include criteria on how Member States can relieve energy-intensive companies that are particularly exposed to international competition from charges levied for the support of renewables. The guidelines allow for reducing the burden for a limited number of energy-intensive sectors defined for the entire EU.
3   To include new provisions on aid to generation capacity so as to strengthen the internal energy market and ensure security of supply.

Opportunities and challenges: network infrastructure and flexibility

To achieve the overall renewable target of 20% in 2020, as well as the differentiated national targets, it is not only relevant to set the right incentives.

It is also important to improve infrastructure, such as the electricity network. In terms of location, the supply of renewable energy may not always match demand. If the wind is strong in Denmark but demand is high in Bavaria in Southern Germany or in Poland, then adequate electricity connections are needed. It is also necessary to ensure that annual or daily peaks in power consumption can be absorbed either by enabling storage or by using more flexible power generation that can be switched on and off quickly.

The emergence of large amounts of variable electricity generation requires a need to move towards a more interconnected, smart and flexible electricity system. This will have very profound impacts on the functioning of electricity markets in the EU. For instance, greater flexibility can be achieved by a further development of shorter-term markets, such as intra-day and balancing markets, so as to ensure the right price signals reward short-term flexibility.

Conventional power is currently confronted with a series of issues in this transition: reduced demand due to the economic recession and the build-up of alternative capacity, the need to provide higher flexibility but for a reduced number of load-hours, and the 'mothballing' of gas plants that are not competitive compared to coal and lignite. Some Member States have therefore opted to introduce, or are considering introducing, capacity mechanisms. This, however, raises the same questions regarding how to prevent potential fragmentation of the internal energy market and potential distortions of competition, while ensuring generation adequacy.

Opportunities and challenges: interactions between policy instruments

There are also implications for the operation of the EU ETS. On the one hand, the renewables legislation will contribute towards meeting the greenhouse gas reductions agreed both in the sectors covered by the EU ETS and those outside the ETS (such as transport). On the other hand, the renewable subsidies increase the use of renewable energy beyond what they would otherwise have been, and so they reduce demand for EU ETS allowances – thereby exerting a downward pressure on carbon prices.

There is, however, a more fundamental question at hand. A high target for renewables might lead to higher (implicit) costs for reducing greenhouse gas emissions than strictly necessary (Marcantonini and Ellermann, 2013;

and Marcantonini and Ellermann, 2014). The argument runs that cheaper options, such as energy efficiency measures, demand-side management, or fuel switching from coal to gas, may not have been fully used, but instead may be replaced by more expensive options such as some forms of renewable energy.

This argument indicates that the approach of the Renewable Energy Sources Directive was quite different from the one followed by the EU ETS. In the latter case full harmonisation at EU-level was pursued for reasons related to the cost-effectiveness of climate policy, while the promotion of renewable energy followed a reasoning of national governance, pursuing potentially various benefits such as greenhouse gas reduction, energy mix preferences, industrial policy and local employment opportunities. The ETS is technology neutral as to which low-carbon route was preferred by economic operators, while the renewable energy approach was by definition technology specific.

Some analysis suggests that the costs for the EU of meeting its 20% greenhouse gas reduction target in 2020 may have been some 10% higher than what was strictly necessary (Capros et al., 2011). This is due to the fact that other options, such as energy efficiency or fuel switching might ultimately have been cheaper. These extra costs can, however, be defended by the additional benefits that renewables bring in terms of reducing dependency on oil and gas imports, and in terms of the advantages gained by developing new technologies (innovation) through learning-by-doing. Moreover, the policies that drive the demand for these technologies may lead to a first-mover advantage in the diffusion of technologies that raises exports, GDP and employment (Pollit et al., 2015).

These are very relevant questions for the design of a revised Renewable Energy Sources Directive that will implement the decision of the European Council of October 2014 to increase the objective to 'at least 27% . . . binding at EU level'. This is in line with the commitment of the EU to become the world leader in renewable energy. This will require the development of the next generation of advanced, competitive renewables energies. Costs have been reduced significantly due to past EU commitment. Moreover renewable production needs to be progressively and efficiently integrated into the internal energy market and energy markets and grids needs to be made fit for renewables.[19] More interconnection and flexibility (flexible supply, including storage and demand–response) will have to be deployed so as to allow for a full use of the potential renewable energy can offer.

Conclusion: the EU policy on renewables has been successful in increasing the share of renewables in final energy consumption from 8.5% in 2005 to 15% in 2015, and is well on track to deliver the target of 20% by 2020. The EU-wide renewable energy target of at least 27% in 2030 as agreed by the European Council is an important signal to the investor community that renewable energy will be an increasingly important and mainstream energy source. Most notably in electricity some 45% will be renewable in 2030. This is challenging but achievable. Finally and crucially, renewable energy will need to be fully integrated into the EU's internal energy market.

Improving energy efficiency

Dependence and barriers

Concerns persist that the EU will be increasingly reliant on imported energy. In 2012, 86% of oil and 66% of gas was imported and by 2030 imports could even increase to 94% for oil and 83% for gas. In addition, even if oil prices have gone down significantly in recent months, energy may also become more expensive over the course of time. The risk of supply interruptions continues because energy imports (especially of oil and gas) are anticipated to come from an increasingly limited number of supplying countries, while domestic production, for example, in the Netherlands and the North Sea, is expected to decline.

Moderating energy demand is one of the options to increase security of supply, as well as being a means to reduce greenhouse gas emissions. The good news is that technological progress in the field of energy efficiency has been considerable, be it in the field of buildings, cars, appliances, or in industry.

But a number of market barriers prevent the development and diffusion of these technologies. Such barriers might be imperfect information on the costs and benefits of energy saving measures, the existence of split incentives (where owners are reluctant to invest in energy savings measures which would benefit the tenant through reduced energy bills), and the lack of knowledge on actual energy consumption or difficulty financing large upfront investments. Individual consumers may pay higher interest rates than assumed for the economy in general. These elements typically lead to underinvestment in energy efficiency compared to what could be regarded as optimal from a social point of view. Such market barriers are not necessarily overcome by setting a price on emissions or by high energy prices.

There are, therefore, strong arguments for government intervention and regulation mainly at Member State level but also at EU level. As part of the climate and energy package of 2009, a non-binding energy efficiency target was agreed. The target is to reduce gross primary energy consumption in 2020 by 20% compared to the 1,842 million tonnes of oil equivalent (Mtoe) level that was expected for 2020 under the 'business-as-usual' projection made in 2007. The latest projections based on additional measures adopted suggest that a reduction of 17% or perhaps even 18–19% may be achieved[20] (Capros et al., 2014).

Regulating the energy use of products and devices

EU-level intervention is especially relevant when it comes to the energy use of products and devices that are traded internationally. One central element is the 'Ecodesign Directive'.[21] This is a European Directive to regulate the design, from an environmental perspective, of products that use energy. All kinds of electrical and electronic equipment are covered, including heating equipment.

The purpose of the legislation is the provision of coherent rules for 'ecodesign' within the European Union so that differences in national laws pose no obstacles to intra-EU trade. The Directive offers a framework to set minimum energy efficiency standards that have to be met for new appliances. Conditions and criteria can also be defined for relevant environmental characteristics for specific products. These can, for example, be criteria relating to water consumption of the product, waste production or the extension of the lifespan of a product. By means of the specific implementing measures the EU seeks to affect the design of electrical and electronic products with a view to their swift and efficient improvement.

Over recent years, within this legal framework, many specific implementing measures have been taken. Table 3.2 gives an overview of the measures that have already been taken so far to improve the energy use of products. An order of magnitude of their expected impact on CO_2 emissions is given as well as an estimated cost impact. Cost estimates are the subject of discussion because they are sensitive to the discount rate used and the expected change of prices over time. The study by Irrek et al. (2010) for example, shows that using 2% real discount rates may make the annual net cost savings between 0 and 50% higher. For example, for office and street lighting cost savings vary between €3.3 billion (4% discount rate) and €1.7 billion (8% discount rate) per year.

TABLE 3.2 Impacts in 2020 of energy efficiency measures under the Ecodesign Directive

Implemented measures	Regulation number	Emission reduction (MtCO₂)	Energy saved (PJ)	Cost saved (billion €/yr)
Non-directional household lamps	244/2009	11	122	3.1
Office & street lighting: fluorescent lamps	245/2009	15	137	2.5
Electric motors	640/2009	64	500	16.8
Televisions	642/2009	17	169	2.3
Complex set top boxes	Voluntary agreement	2	16	0.6
Simple set top boxes	107/2009	2	17	0.7
External power supplies & battery chargers	278/2009	4	118	0.5
Standby & off modus losses	1275/2008	11	128	2.1
Domestic refrigerators & freezers	643/2009	1	14	0.5
Circulators pumps for heating	641/2009 &622/2009	12	96	3.9
Domestic dish washers	1016/2010 &1015/2010	1	7	−0.1
Domestic washing machines	1016/2010 &1015/2010	1	5	−0.1
Industrial fans	327/2011	25	487	7.1
Room air conditioners	206/2012	4	41	0.7
Water pumps	547/2012	1	10	0.3
Household tumble driers	932/2012	2	12	0.2
Directional lamps & LED lamps	1194/2012	10	89	1.3
Computers and servers	617/2013	9	74	2.3
Vacuum cleaners	666/2013	6	68	2.8
Standby and off mode power of equipment	801/2013	11	128	2.8
Space & combination heaters	813/2013	109	1,884	25.4
Water heaters	814/2013	26	453	4.4

(Continued)

TABLE 3.2 (Continued)

Implemented measures	Regulation number	Emission reduction (MtCO$_2$)	Energy saved (PJ)	Cost saved (billion €/yr)
Imaging equipment	Voluntary agreement	4	15	9.2
Domestic cooking appliances	66/2014	1	27	−0.6
SUM		348	4,617	88.9
Of which electricity		198	2,099	56

Sources: Irrek et al. (2010) and Specific Impact Assessments under the Ecodesign Directive.

Bearing in mind the above caveats, Table 3.2 shows that the expected impacts of this Directive could be significant. The table is based on the analysis of the preferred option which may differ from the precise formulation finally agreed by the Member States.[22] The 22 specific Regulations and two Voluntary Agreements agreed as of 2014 are expected to reduce the EU's greenhouse gas emissions by nearly 350 million tonnes of CO_2-equivalent (MtCO$_2$eq.) in 2020. Noteworthy is that 40% of the energy savings comes from only one measure: improving the efficiency of space and combination heaters (heat and hot water) (see Table 3.2). Major contributions are also made by efficiency improvements of electric motors, industrial fans and water heaters. The Ecodesign Directive's estimated impact corresponds to a 7% reduction in electricity demand in 2020.

As Table 3.2 illustrates, the measures are generally expected to result in net cost savings, since the energy costs saved outweigh the expected additional investment and possible operating and maintenance costs. There are three exceptions, however, where there are additional net costs rather than net cost savings, and these are all in the household appliances sector: dish washers, washing machines and cooking appliances.

Since 1992 there is also a Directive for a European energy label.[23] The energy label is a tool to assist consumers when purchasing household appliances, such as washing machines and dishwashers. The categories 'A' to 'G' show to what extent the product is economical and environmentally friendly. In providing a clearer regulatory framework for industry, the Directive increases the amount of information available to consumers on the energy use of products, enabling more informed choice and lower energy bills, as well as reducing CO_2 emissions in the EU.

Importantly, in 2010 the Directive on the energy performance of buildings was reviewed.[24] Residential and commercial buildings are large users of energy and buildings account for some 40% of energy consumption in the EU. Under this Directive, Member States must establish and apply minimum energy performance requirements for new and existing buildings, ensure the certification of these energy performance requirements and ensure the regular inspection of boilers and air-conditioning systems in buildings. Moreover, the Directive requires Member States to ensure that by 2021 all new buildings are so-called 'nearly zero-energy buildings'. The recasting in 2010 of the Directive is expected to reduce energy consumption by 60–80 Mtoe, and reduce CO_2 emissions by 5% in 2020. It could also create 280,000 to 450,000 new jobs in the building sector that in total employs around 8 million people in the EU.

The Energy Efficiency Directive of 2012

On top of the initiatives on ecodesign, energy labelling and the energy performance of buildings, a new Energy Efficiency Directive was adopted in 2012.[25] The main purpose was to make a significant contribution to meeting the EU's 2020 energy efficiency target of 20%. The Directive includes a wide range of policy measures, and covers residential energy efficiency, smart meters, home energy management, energy audits in the commercial sector, retrofitting of public buildings, district heating as well as demand response.

The main elements of the Directive are the following:

1   Member States have to establish a long-term strategy for the renovation of residential and commercial buildings. They also need to renovate 3% of the floor area of public buildings owned by central governments.
2   Central governments must buy only products, services and buildings that have high energy efficiency 'insofar as this is consistent with cost-effectiveness, economic feasibility, wider sustainability, technical suitability, as well as sufficient competition'.
3   Member States have to introduce legislation that obliges energy distribution companies to achieve cumulative end-use savings of on average 1.5% a year of energy sales to final consumers between 2014 and 2020.
4   Large enterprises must undergo energy audits at least every four years. Audits for small- and medium-sized enterprises must be promoted by governments.
5   Billing in homes must be based on actual, rather than estimated, energy consumption by 2015.
6   Member States have to assess the potential for cogeneration, district heating and cooling by 2015, and thereafter every five years.

Article 7, introducing energy savings obligations on energy suppliers or distributors of the Directive is the most innovative, since it could make energy suppliers *de facto* 'suppliers' of energy-efficient services and products. Nearly half of the energy savings from the Directive are expected to come from this Article alone.[26] Flexibilities are allowed in meeting these energy saving obligations by energy suppliers and distributors, and the Directive also allows Member States to adopt equivalent measures that meet the same energy savings as an alternative. Overall the Directive is estimated to reduce energy consumption by 58 Mtoe equivalent. This is expected to result in a 12% reduction in energy consumption compared to the 2007 baseline.

The European Council, at its meeting of October 2014, decided to continue efforts to improve energy efficiency and decided on 'an indicative target at the EU level of at least 27% in 2030. This will be reviewed by 2020, having in mind an EU level of 30%.' The 27% is expressed as a reduction of the gross inland consumption of energy in the EU compared to the business-as-usual (reference) projection made in 2007. Particularly in the light of lower than expected fossil fuel prices in 2014, 2015 and possibly beyond, it can be expected that policies will continue to be needed to ensure performance beyond business-as-usual (Capros et al., 2014).

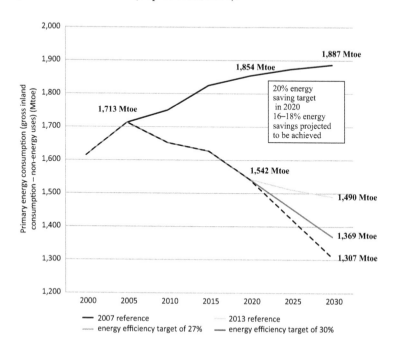

FIGURE 3.4 EU-2030 target: at least 27% energy savings in 2030

Conclusion: improving energy efficiency has become a key contributor in reducing greenhouse gas emissions. The EU adopted an indicative target of 20% below a predetermined baseline for 2020, and although clear progress has been made, it will be difficult to meet. Because of other important benefits, not least in terms of security of supply, improving the trade balance, and creating job opportunities in the construction sector, the European Council decided to step-up efforts and agreed upon an indicative energy efficiency target of 27% by 2030.

Emissions from cars, vans, lorries and ships

Introduction

Approximately one fifth of the total greenhouse gas emissions in the EU come from the transport sector, and these are expected to continue growing up to 2050, but at a reduced rate. These emissions are covered by the Effort Sharing Decision (which regulates greenhouse gas emissions in the EU that are not covered by the EU ETS – see Chapter 4) representing around half of the EU's greenhouse gas emissions including transport. Regulating transport emissions is therefore essential to meeting the non-ETS targets.

Regulating emissions from cars and vans

Initially, emission standards for the average emissions of new passenger cars were fixed in Voluntary Agreements with car manufacturers, notably to reach 140 grams per kilometre (g/km) by 2008/2009. That did not function well in practice, as the targets were not met. Since 2009, these emissions standards have therefore been set in binding legislation[27] so as to create clarity and regulatory certainty. All new passenger cars registered in the EU in 2015 and 2021 shall emit on average an emission standard of 130 and 95 g CO_2/km respectively. Heavier cars may emit more than lighter cars but the average of all new cars sold by each manufacturer must reach the set target.

The 2015 and 2021 targets represent reductions of 18% and 40% respectively compared with the 2007 fleet average of 158.7 g/km. In terms of fuel consumption, the 2015 target is approximately equivalent to 5.6 litres per 100 kilometres (ltr/100 km) of petrol or 4.9 ltr/100 km of diesel. The 2021 target equates to approximately 4.1 ltr/100 km of petrol or 3.6 ltr/100 km of diesel. Car manufacturers have been innovating with a variety of technologies and succeeded in reaching the 130 g target well before the date of delivery

(EEA, 2012). This contrasts with the average of 186 g in 1995 and 173 g CO_2/km in the year 2000.

In 2011 and in 2014[28] the EU adopted legislation to reduce CO_2 emissions from light-duty vehicles setting CO_2 emission targets for new vans sold on the European market. The obligations are comparable to those relating to new passenger cars. The Regulation limits CO_2 emissions from new vans to a fleet average of 175 g CO_2 per kilometre by 2017 and 147 g/km by 2020. These targets represent reductions of 3% and 19% respectively compared with the 2012 average of 180.2 g CO_2/km. This Regulation is expected to reduce fuel consumption to 5.5 ltr/100 km for diesel-fuelled vans by 2020.

Important to note are the flexibilities allowed for compliance purposes with the targets for new passenger cars. The 95 g CO_2/km target in 2021 allows for the use of special incentives ('super credits'). The 'super credits' apply to cars with emissions below 50 g CO_2/km, such as electric or plug-in hybrid cars. Such low-emitting cars will be counted as 2 vehicles in 2020, 1.67 in 2021, 1.33 in 2022 and as 1 vehicle from 2023. This will incentivise manufacturers to develop and deploy new technologies that could help further reduce the average emissions of the new car fleet. The contribution of these 'super credits' will be capped and the credits can only make a contribution of 7.5 g/km for each car manufacturer between 2020 and 2022. There are also specific provisions for smaller manufacturers of fewer than 10,000 vehicles per year, and producers of fewer than 1,000 cars per year are exempted.

If we compare the EU policy with that of other countries, both Japan and the EU appear currently to be world leaders based on a study on the average emissions in grams per kilometre per passenger car. Figure 3.5 shows the emission standards for passenger cars in a number of countries.[29] In 2002, the average emissions of new passenger cars in the EU and Japan were well below that of other countries. Countries like the United States and China are catching up quickly, closely followed by others, including Canada and Korea. From 2020, however, the EU is expected to have the strictest fuel efficiency standard of 4.1 ltr/100 km (in effect from 2021 onwards), followed closely by Japan (4.5 ltr/100 km) and India and China (4.8 and 5 ltr/100 km respectively).

It is remarkable that despite the fact these policies have developed quite independently from each other, today 75% of global car sales are subject to some form of CO_2 or energy efficiency legislation, and that the stringency of these policies is converging.

In addition to the emission limit values, an EU Directive is in place that ensures that consumers buying a new passenger car receive information about

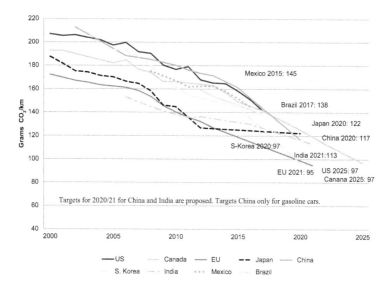

FIGURE 3.5 Average emission standards for new passenger cars in the world (US and Canada values are for light duty vehicles)

Note: Adapted from: ICCT.

fuel consumption and CO_2 emissions of the specific car.[30] This labelling is essential for consumers to make informed choices, as it cannot be simply assumed that they have ready access to this information.

Emissions from heavy-duty vehicles

While passenger car emissions are now subject to EU legislation, this is not yet the case for heavy-duty vehicles (HDV), such as trucks and buses. CO_2 emissions from HDV have increased by around 36% between 1990 and 2010 and are expected to more or less remain at this level until 2050.[31]

A core issue is that CO_2 emissions from HDV are neither measured nor certified or recorded when new vehicles are registered. Technically speaking, CO_2 emissions from new HDV could be reduced by at least 30% in a cost-effective way. However, a number of market barriers prevent the uptake of these measures: few companies have data to evaluate the fuel efficiency of new HDV; HDV producers offer fewer fuel-saving technology options; operators use high discount rates when making decisions, expecting returns on investment within three years rather than over the technical lifetime of 11 years; or split incentives between the owner of the vehicle (a leasing company, for example) and the operator who would benefit from lower fuel costs.[32] For the above reasons, the Commission proposed in May 2014 that first action is needed to improve knowledge of the actual fuel consumption of HDV using a new methodology, as well as on certifying and reporting CO_2 emissions of new vehicles, as was done for passenger cars previously. Once this is implemented, further action may be considered.

Addressing greenhouse gas emissions from shipping

The annual global CO_2 emissions from shipping exceed 870 million tonnes, and these are accompanied by emissions of black carbon that are believed to have significant climate impacts, in particular in the Arctic. The CO_2 emissions from journeys between ports in the EU, and to and from the ports outside the EU, are expected to reach 210 million tonnes of CO_2 by 2020.[33] By 2050, without action, global emissions from shipping are expected to more than double from current levels.

The EU's climate policy for shipping is similar in a number of ways to aviation: there is a UN organisation, the International Maritime Organization (IMO), with a good track record of adopting technical and operational measures. At the same time, a number of third countries have expressed concern about any measure not adopted by global consensus. Compared to aviation, however, a major difference is that the quality of data for shipping emissions is generally poor, with levels of uncertainty up to approximately 20%. Moreover, many cost-saving CO_2 reduction measures in the maritime transport sector are not being implemented, in part due to market barriers such as a lack of information, access to finance and split incentives.

Against this background, in June 2013 the Commission published a Strategy for addressing maritime emissions,[34] and at the same time proposed a Regulation of the European Parliament and of the Council on the monitoring, reporting and verification of greenhouse gas emissions from shipping.[35] This proposal has been agreed by the European Parliament and the Council as Regulation (EU) 2015/757, of 29 April 2015.[36] Rather than proposing market-based measures, such as the inclusion of shipping into the EU ETS, the Commission considered it more appropriate to progress in a step-wise manner, given the importance of a robust system of measuring emissions. A system of monitoring, reporting and verification (MRV) by itself is expected to reduce costs by increasing information and transparency on fuel use, and to highlight the potential for cost-effective emission reductions. The EU's measure is explicitly intended to facilitate adoption of comparable MRV standards within the IMO, and is enabling better insights into the potential of the sector to reduce its emissions.

Conclusion: emissions from new cars have been successfully reduced in the EU through setting mandatory standards and this triggered accelerated innovation in the automotive sector. Fuel consumption of cars is projected to fall year by year to an average consumption of not more than 4.1 litres per 100 km by 2021. Vans follow a similar path of improvement. From a global perspective similar regulation has been introduced in all major regions of the world. For lorries and emissions from shipping, the first emphasis has been put on establishing a solid monitoring of emissions.

Outlook

This chapter started with an assessment of the current way that the EU produces and consumes energy, concluding that for the moment it is neither sustainable, nor secure or competitive. It also clearly indicated the important role that Member States play in designing policies in this field, in particular when energy security is at stake.

Enhancing the role of renewable energy is an important aspect of the EU's strategy in this respect, and the EU appears to be well on the way to meeting its target of a 20% share of renewable energy by 2020. Compared to 10 years ago, where renewable energy was a niche market in a few countries, the prospect of many renewable energy sources being competitive with mainstream technology is no longer a distant dream but a reality that needs to be addressed.

The rapid development of renewable energy, notably in the power sector, the cost reductions and the increasing globalisation of the industry is bringing major new challenges. How should the EU adapt its regulatory framework that governs the EU internal market so as to enable a more interconnected, smart and flexible electricity system? How can regional cooperation contribute? How should the EU remain a leader in renewable energy and keep, or regain, a first-mover advantage in the face of aggressive industrial policies in other parts of the world? It is these questions that are also at the heart of the Energy Union strategy paper launched by the European Commission in February 2015.

On energy efficiency, a collection of policies has been introduced: efficiency measures under the Ecodesign Directive, CO_2 Regulations for passenger cars and vans, the Energy Performance of Buildings Directive and the Energy Efficiency Directive. These measures will reduce energy consumption compared to the projections, but reaching the target of reducing energy consumption by 20% in 2020 and by 27% in 2030 below the business-as-usual forecast of 2007 will still require enhanced efforts.

Irrespective of whether the indicative target will be met or not, progress in energy efficiency has been remarkable. Most notably, efficiency standards for appliances and legislation for cars have been shown to trigger accelerated product innovation. An important lesson for the future may be that such legislation that directly regulates particular sectors in an internal market of more than 500 million consumers, is effective, and can lead to significant results.

Another element is the link to global developments. Despite quite independent regulatory developments, and indeed the lack of any real coordination, such as could have been triggered by an ambitious international climate agreement, we see a dissemination and replication of policies throughout the world, not least in major emerging economies. This is certainly an encouraging sign. This has led to a situation that in some areas, such as renewable energy, emerging economies are now bigger markets than the developed world.

In addition, global competition in energy innovation has been increasing steadily. As other countries have identified the potential benefits of new technology for their economy, they also strive towards technological leadership. This is very important for Europe, as renewable energy, the automotive sector (and transport technology more generally), industrial and household equipment are all strongholds of the European manufacturing sector. The growth in global 'clean-tech' therefore provides a major growth opportunity for European companies, but realising this opportunity will require strenuous efforts in the light of international competition.

In parallel with all the developments in the energy field of such relevance to the EU's climate policies, the EU's energy security strategy[37] has undoubtedly received new impetus as a result of the tensions between Russia and Ukraine. This only underlines the need for ambitious energy and climate policies in the decade up to 2030. The moderation of energy demand is indeed a central pillar of the EU as well as a most important contribution to meet the EU's climate goals.

Finally, this chapter has shown that the EU has more work to do on energy policy so as to make it sustainable, secure and competitive. It remains, however, the EU's belief that it is in its long-term interests to develop alternative low-carbon or carbon-free energy sources that will in time become price competitive with fossil-generated energy. The cost curves of many renewable energy technologies continue to fall, while the price of polluting must increasingly be made to reflect all externalities. The 'crossing point', when renewable energies become equal to or lower in cost than conventional energy, will occur for different technologies at different times. The EU's climate and energy policy frameworks now being put in place, in conjunction with Member State policies, are focused on bringing forward in time this 'crossing point', thereby providing greater resilience and competitiveness to the EU economy.

In the meantime, keeping climate and energy policies as cost-effective as possible is crucial. Evidence of this realisation can be seen in the evolution of climate and energy policies over time, with increasing emphasis on flexibilities in complying with EU legislation and goals, and on the minimisation of inconsistencies between instruments. It is important to see the 2030 climate and energy policy framework, as endorsed by the European Council, in this light. The 2030 framework comprises fewer binding national targets, no 'sub-targets' such as exist to 2020 for transport, and greater flexibilities for Member States to choose what is right for them. This gradual evolution of policy is evidence once again of the EU's learning-by-doing, and the gradual improvement of both the effectiveness and cost-effectiveness of policies over time.

Notes

1   Eurostat (2014) EU Energy in figures Statistical Pocketbook 2014; pp. 66, 70 and 72: http://ec.europa.eu/energy/sites/ener/files/documents/2014_pocketbook.pdf
2   European Commission (2011) Energy Roadmap 2050, COM(2011) 885 final of 15.12.2011: http://eur-lex.europa.eu/legal-content/EN/TXT/PDF/?uri=CELEX:52011DC0885&rid=3
3   European Commission (2015): 'A Framework Strategy for a Resilient Energy Union with a Forward-Looking Climate Change Policy', COM(2015) 80 final dated 25.2.2015: http://ec.europa.eu/priorities/energy-union/docs/energyunion_en.pdf
4   Directive 2009/28/EC of the European Parliament and of the Council of 23 April 2009 on the promotion of the use of energy from renewable sources and amending and subsequently repealing Directives 2001/77/EC and 2003/30/EC; OJ L 140, 5.6.2009, pp. 16–62: http://eur-lex.europa.eu/legal-content/EN/TXT/PDF/?uri=CELEX:32009L0028&from=en
5   Notably in Article 6(3) of the Commission's original Proposal: http://eur-lex.europa.eu/legal-content/EN/TXT/PDF/?uri=CELEX:52008PC0019&from=EN
6   European Commission (2013) Renewable energy progress report, 27.3.2013. COM(2013) 175 final: http://eur-lex.europa.eu/legal-content/EN/TXT/PDF/?uri=CELEX:52013DC0175&from=EN
7   Source: Eurostat News Release 43/2015 – 10 March 2015: http://ec.europa.eu/eurostat/documents/2995521/6734513/8–10032015-AP-EN.pdf/3a8c018d-3d9f-4f1d-95ad-832ed3a20a6b

8 Source of graphic: http://ec.europa.eu/eurostat/statistics-explained/images/e/
   e5/F_RENEWABLES_ENERGY_FOR_FINAL_CONSUMPTION_2012.png
9 See Bloomberg http://about.bnef.com/summit/content/uploads/sites/3/2013/
   12/2013-04-23-BNEF-Summit-2013-keynote-presentation-Michael-
   Liebreich-BNEF-Chief-Executive.pdf. Also see JRC (2014).
10 See IRENA 'Summary for Policy Makers: Renewable Power Generation Costs',
   November 2012: www.irena.org/DocumentDownloads/Publications/Renew-
   able_Power_Generation_Costs.pdf (consulted 17/04/2015).
11 Directive 2009/30/EC of the European Parliament and of the Council of
   23.4.2009 amending Directive 98/70/EC as regards the specification of petrol,
   diesel and gas-oil and introducing a mechanism to monitor and reduce greenhouse
   gas emissions and amending Council Directive 1999/32/EC as regards the specification of fuel used by inland waterway vessels and repealing Directive 93/12/
   EEC; OJ L 140, 5.6.2009, pp. 88–113: http://eur-lex.europa.eu/legal-content/
   EN/TXT/PDF/?uri=CELEX:32009L0030&from=EN
12 European Commission (2013) 'Renewable energy progress report' COM(2013)
   175 final of 27 March 2013, p. 6: http://eur-lex.europa.eu/legal-content/EN/
   TXT/PDF/?uri=CELEX:52013DC0175&from=EN
13 Eurostat (2014) EU Energy in figures Statistical Pocketbook 2014; p. 114: http://
   ec.europa.eu/energy/sites/ener/files/documents/2014_pocketbook.pdf
14 See Eurostat http://ec.europa.eu/eurostat/statistics explained/index.php/File:
   Share_of_energy_from_renewable_sources_in_transport_-_2013.png (consulted
   6.5.2015).
15 European Commission (2013) 'Renewable energy progress report', Commission Staff Working Document, SWD(2013) 102 final, 27 March 2013, pp. 27–28:
   http://eur-lex.europa.eu/legal-content/EN/TXT/PDF/?uri=CELEX:52013D
   C0175&from=EN
16 European Commission (2014) 'A policy framework for climate and energy in
   the period from 2020 to 2030' COM(2014)15 final of 22.1.2014; Communication from the Commission to the European Parliament, the Council, the Economic and Social Committee and the Committee of the Regions: http://eur-lex.
   europa.eu/legal-content/EN/TXT/PDF/?uri=CELEX:52014DC0015&from
   =EN with further information at: http://ec.europa.eu/clima/policies/2030/
   documentation_en.htm
17 In particular, pages 9 and 13 of European Commission (2013) 'Renewable energy
   progress report', COM(2013) 175 final of 27 March 2013: http://eur-lex.europa.
   eu/legal-content/EN/TXT/PDF/?uri=CELEX:52013DC0175&from=EN
18 European Commission (2014) 'Guidelines on State aid for environmental protection and energy 2014–2020', Communication, OJ C 200, 28.6.2014, pp. 1–55:
   http://eur-lex.europa.eu/legal-content/EN/TXT/PDF/?uri=CELEX:52014X
   C0628%2801%29&from=EN
19 European Commission (2015) 'A Framework Strategy for a Resilient Energy Union
   with a Forward-Looking Climate Change Policy', COM(2015) 80 final dated
   25.2.2015: http://ec.europa.eu/priorities/energy-union/docs/energyunion_en.pdf
20 European Commission, (2014) 'Energy efficiency and its contribution to energy
   security and the 2030 Framework for climate and energy policy', Communication,

European Commission, COM(2014) 520 final, 23.7.2014: http://ec.europa.eu/
energy/sites/ener/files/documents/2014_eec_communication_adopted_0.pdf

21 Directive 2009/125/EC of the European Parliament and of the Council of 21
October 2009 establishing a framework for the setting of ecodesign requirements
for energy-related products; OJ L 285, 31.10.2009, pp. 10–35: http://eur-lex.
europa.eu/legal-content/EN/TXT/PDF/?uri=CELEX:32009L0125&from=EN

22 See http://ec.europa.eu/energy/efficiency/ecodesign/doc/overview_legislation_
eco-design.pdf (consulted 23.5.2014).

23 Directive 2010/30/EU of the European Parliament and of the Council of 19
May 2010 on the indication by labelling and standard product information of the
consumption of energy and other resources by energy-related products; OJ L 153,
18.6.2010, pp. 1–12: http://eur-lex.europa.eu/legal-content/EN/TXT/PDF/?ur
i=CELEX:32010L0030&from=EN

24 Directive 2010/31/EU of the European Parliament and of the Council of 19
May 2010 on the energy performance of buildings; OJ L 153, 18.6.2010,
pp. 13–35: http://eur-lex.europa.eu/legal-content/EN/TXT/PDF/?uri=CELE
X:32010L0031&from=EN

25 Directive 2012/27/EU of the European Parliament and of the Council of 25
October 2012 on energy efficiency, amending Directives 2009/125/EC and
2010/30/EU and repealing Directives 2004/8/EC and 2006/32/EC; OJ L 315,
14.11.2012, pp. 1–56: http://eur-lex.europa.eu/legal-content/EN/TXT/PDF/?
uri=CELEX:32012L0027&from=EN

26 European Commission (2012) Non-paper of the services of the European Commission on energy efficiency Directive, Informal Energy Council, 19–20 April 2012:
http://ec.europa.eu/energy/en/content/non-paper-energy-efficiency-directive
(consulted 21.4.2015).

27 Regulation (EC) No. 443/2009 of the European Parliament and of the Council of 23 April 2009 setting emission performance standards for new passenger
cars as part of the Community's integrated approach to reduce CO_2 emissions
from light-duty vehicles; OJ L 140, 5.6.2009, pp. 1–25: http://eur-lex.europa.
eu/legal-content/EN/TXT/PDF/?uri=CELEX:02009R0443–20130508&from
=EN and Regulation (EU) No. 333/2014 of the European Parliament and of
the Council of 11 March 2014 amending Regulation (EC) No. 443/2009 to
define the modalities for reaching the 2020 target to reduce CO_2 emissions from
new passenger cars; OJ L 103, 5.4.2014, pp. 15–21: http://eur-lex.europa.eu/
legal-content/EN/TXT/PDF/?uri=CELEX:32014R0333&from=EN

28 Regulation (EU) No. 510/2011 of the European Parliament and of the Council
of 11 May 2011 setting emission performance standards for new light commercial vehicles as part of the Union's integrated approach to reduce CO_2 emissions
from light-duty vehicles; OJ L 145, 31.5.2011, pp. 1–18: http://eur-lex.europa.
eu/legal-content/EN/TXT/PDF/?uri=CELEX:32011R0510&from=EN; and
Regulation (EU) No. 253/2014 of the European Parliament and of the Council
of 26 February 2014 amending Regulation (EU) No. 510/2011 to define the
modalities for reaching the 2020 target to reduce CO_2 emissions from new light
commercial vehicles; OJ L 84, 20.3.2014, pp. 38–41: http://eur-lex.europa.eu/
legal-content/EN/TXT/PDF/?uri=CELEX:32014R0253&from=EN

29 Based on data from the ICCT, see: www.theicct.org/info-tools/global-passenger-vehicle-standards (consulted 21.4.2015).

30 Directive 1999/94/EC of the European Parliament and of the Council of 13 December 1999 relating to the availability of consumer information on fuel economy and CO_2 emissions in respect of the marketing of new passenger cars; OJ L12, 18.1.2000, pp. 16–23: http://eur-lex.europa.eu/legal-content/EN/TXT/PDF/?uri=CELEX:31999L0094&from=EN

31 European Commission (2014) 'Strategy for reducing Heavy-Duty Vehicles' fuel consumption and CO_2 emissions' COM(2104) 285 final, 21.5.2014: http://ec.europa.eu/clima/policies/transport/vehicles/heavy/docs/com_285_2014_en.pdf (more information is available on the European Commission's website at: http://ec.europa.eu/clima/policies/transport/vehicles/heavy/documentation_en.htm).

32 European Commission (2014) 'Executive Summary of the Impact Assessment of a Strategy for Reducing Heavy-Duty Vehicles' fuel consumption and CO_2 emissions', Commission Staff Working Document reference: SWD(2014) 159 final, 21.5.2014: http://ec.europa.eu/clima/policies/transport/vehicles/heavy/docs/swd_2014_159_en.pdf (consulted 22.4.2015).

33 European Commission (2013) Impact Assessment – Part 1, Commission Staff Working Document Accompanying the document 'Proposal for a Regulation of the European Parliament and of the Council on the monitoring, reporting and verification of carbon dioxide emissions from maritime transport and amending Regulation (EU) No. 525/2013' (COM(2013) 480 final) (SWD(2013) 236 final, Brussels of 28.6.2013. SWD(2013) 237 final/2: http://ec.europa.eu/clima/policies/transport/shipping/docs/swd_2013_237_1_en.pdf

34 European Commission (2013) 'Integrating maritime transport emissions in the EU's greenhouse gas reduction policies' COM(2013) 479 of 28.6.2013: http://ec.europa.eu/clima/policies/transport/shipping/docs/com_2013_479_en.pdf

35 Proposal for a Regulation of the European Parliament and of the Council on the monitoring, reporting and verification of carbon dioxide emissions from maritime transport and amending Regulation (EU) No. 525/2013, COM(2013) 480 final of 28.6.2013: http://ec.europa.eu/clima/policies/transport/shipping/docs/com_2013_480_en.pdf

36 See http://eur-lex.europa.eu/legal-content/EN/TXT/PDF/?uri=OJ:JOL_2015_123_R_0007&from=EN

37 European Commission (2014) 'European Energy Security Strategy' COM(2014) 330 final of 28.5.2014: http://eur-lex.europa.eu/legal-content/EN/TXT/PDF/?uri=CELEX:52014DC0330&from=EN

References

Capros, P., Mantzos, L., Parousos, L., Tasios, N., Klaassen, G., and van Ierland, T. (2011) 'Analysis of the EU policy package on climate change and renewables'. *Energy Policy*, 39(3), pp. 1476–1485.

Capros, P., de Vita, A., Tasios, N., Papadopoulos, D., Siskos, P., Apostolaki, E., Zampara, M., Paroussos, L., Fragiadakis, K., Kouvaritakis, N., Hoglund-Isaksson, L.,

Winiwarter, W., Purohit, P., Böttcher, H., Frank, S., Havlik, P., Gusti, M., and Witzke, H. P. (2014) *EU energy, transport and GHG emissions: trends to 2050, reference scenario 2013*. Publications office of the European Union, Luxembourg (http://ec.europa. eu/clima/policies/2030/models/eu_trends_2050_en.pdf), consulted 9/4/2014).

EEA (2012) CO_2 emission performance of car manufacturers in 2011, European Environment Agency, Copenhagen (www.eea.europa.eu//publications/ monitoring-co_2-emissions-from-new).

Eurostat (2014) EU energy in figures Statistical Pocketbook 2014: http://ec.europa. eu/energy/sites/ener/files/documents/2014_pocketbook.pdf

IEA (2012) World Energy Outlook 2012 © OECD/IEA 2012 *World Energy Outlook*, IEA Publishing, Paris, p. 76.

Irrek, W., L. Tholen and M. Franke (2010) Analysis of impact of efficiency standards on EU GHG emissions, Final Task 3 report: outlook on the estimated greenhouse gas emission reductions (Contract EC DGENV), Hamburg, Ökopol. (http://ec.europa.eu/clima/policies/effort/docs/impact_ggas_en.pdf), consulted 26.3.2013.

JRC (2014) 2013 JRC wind status report: 'Technology, market and economic aspects of wind energy in Europe', by Roberto Lacal Arántegui (https://ec.europa.eu/ jrc/sites/default/files/ldna26266enc_2013_jrc_wind_status_report_final.pdf).

JRC (2014a) ETRI 2014 Energy technology reference indicator projections for 2012–2050. JRC Science and Policy reports. Report EUR 26950 EN, Luxembourg, Publication Office of the European Commission.

Klaassen, G., Miketa, A., Larsen, K., and Sundqvist, T. (2005) 'The impact of R&D on innovation for wind energy in Denmark, Germany and the United Kingdom', *Ecological Economics*, 54, pp. 227–240.

Marcantonini, C., and Ellermann, D. (2013) 'The Cost of Abating CO_2 Emissions by Renewable Energy Incentives in Germany'. European University Institute, Florence. EUI Working Paper RSCAS 2013/05: http://cadmus.eui.eu/bitstream/handle/1814/25842/RSCAS_2013_05rev.pdf?sequence=1 (consulted 21.4.2015).

Marcantonini, C., and Ellermann, D. (2014) 'The Implicit Carbon Price of Renewable Energy Incentives in Germany', European University Institute, Florence. EUI Working Paper RSCAS 2014/28: http://cadmus.eui.eu/bitstream/handle/ 1814/30200/RSCAS_2014_28_REV.pdf?sequence=3 (consulted 21 April 2015).

Pollit, H., Summerton, P., and Klaassen, G. (2015) 'A model-based assessment of first-mover advantage and climate policy'. *Environmental Economics and Policy Studies*, 17: 299–312.

Stiglitz, J. (2013) *The Price of Inequality*, New York: W. W. Norton.

4

FRAMING MEMBER STATES' POLICIES

Jos Delbeke and Ger Klaassen

Introduction

The previous two chapters explained the EU's emissions trading system and the contribution energy policy makes to changing energy consumption and reducing greenhouse gas emissions. Other pieces of (non-energy) related EU legislation to address climate change from sectors outside the scope of the EU ETS have not yet been discussed. This is the purpose of this chapter.

The second section starts with a description of the Effort Sharing Decision that determines the emission reductions of greenhouse gas emissions not covered by the ETS. This is followed by EU legislation to control non-CO_2 greenhouse gas emissions, such as the revision of the 'F-gas' Regulation agreed in March 2014. Then, the carbon sources and sinks from land use, land-use change and forestry (LULUCF) are addressed. The chapter closes with a description of EU climate adaptation policy and mainstreaming into the EU budget.

The Effort Sharing Decision for the non-ETS sectors

The sectors outside the ETS constitute around half of the EU's greenhouse gas emissions. Included are the greenhouse gas emissions from smaller industrial installations, services, transport, agriculture, waste and households. The reductions for the non-ETS sectors are made legally binding by the Effort Sharing Decision[1]. Carbon emissions (or carbon sinks) from land use and land-use changes and forestry (LULUCF) are not included under the existing targets for the period up to 2020 set in the Effort Sharing Decision.

The EU target for greenhouse gas reductions in 2020 compared to 1990 is 20%. This implies an emission reduction of around 14% compared to EU greenhouse gas emissions in 2005, 2005 being the first year for which comparable verified emissions data was available for the sectors covered by the EU ETS. The 14% reduction in 2020 was not equally shared between the ETS and non-ETS sectors, since emission reductions were expected to be cheaper in the ETS than in the non-ETS sectors. The reduction agreed for the sectors covered by the EU ETS was 21% compared to 2005 and the reduction for the non-ETS sectors was around 10% compared to 2005. These reduction objectives were based on extended economic analysis (see Delbeke et al., 2010; Capros et al., 2011).

The central element of the Effort Sharing Decision is the fact that emission reductions are distributed between Member States in order to arrive at an efficient and fair sharing of the abatement efforts. The differentiated national targets set by the Effort Sharing Decision are only one part of the overall burden-sharing. The other parts are the redistribution of auctioning revenues and the differentiated renewable energy targets for each Member State. This combination of burden-sharing was intended to ensure a fair sharing of the efforts between the EU Member States, while also maintaining, as much as possible, the incentives to implement cost-effective measures.

Fairness considerations for the distribution of the emission reductions from the non-ETS sectors were based on GDP *per capita* (in 2005). Member States with a lower GDP *per capita* would still be allowed to increase emissions compared to 2005, to allow for catching up. Relatively rich Member States would have to reduce emissions. For example, Bulgaria and Romania were allowed to increase their emissions by 20% compared to 2005, whereas the three richest EU Member States at the time (Denmark, Ireland and Luxembourg) had to reduce emissions by 20% compared to 2005. The remaining Member States had to reduce emissions by percentages between +20% and −20% (see Figure 4.1). Belgium, for example, has to reduce emissions by 15% and the Netherlands by 16% in 2020. The target for Croatia was agreed on the same principles during the accession negotiations.

Member States are responsible for these binding targets and hence have to put in place policies to meet them. However, a number of EU-wide sector-specific measures are in place to assist countries in meeting these targets (see Chapter 3 and the next sections of this chapter).

The targets are set according to the principle of fairness, which was important to gain political acceptability. However, it is legitimate to ask whether this has not been bought at the expense of economic efficiency. Some Member States might, for example, have a high GDP *per capita* but fewer technical (or more expensive) options to reduce emissions. To alleviate this problem

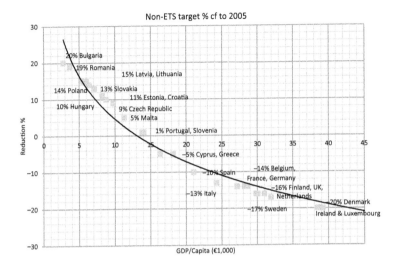

FIGURE 4.1 Sharing the efforts in the non–ETS sectors in relation to GDP *per capita*

the Effort Sharing Decision includes a number of flexibilities. First, Member States may transfer any surplus of their annual emission allocation for a given year to other Member States if their actual emissions are below their predetermined allocation. This would, of course, be done in exchange for financial transfers, or some equivalent benefit. Second, Member States may make limited use of credits from project activities under the Kyoto Protocol (CDM and JI) to meet the national targets, subject to a number of restrictions. These flexibilities would significantly improve the cost-efficiency of the Decision (see, for example, Tol, 2009). Furthermore, these flexibilities are essential in view of the inherent uncertainties around future emissions, resulting from uncertainties linked to the underlying factors causing emissions, such as weather, economic growth and energy prices.

The national targets for 2020 for the non-ETS sectors have been translated in a linear trajectory for the period 2013 to 2020 for the purposes of monitoring of progress over time. The actual setting of annual emission allocations for each Member State for the years 2013 to 2020 was decided separately (see Table 4.1).[2] Table 4.1 gives the numbers for 2013 and 2020 based on the greenhouse gas warming potentials of the second IPCC Assessment Report.

The differentiated allocation of targets per Member State and the precise translation of the targets into annual emission budgets has been a complicated exercise, technically as well as politically. In the international negotiations it is sometimes overlooked how much experience the EU has acquired in reaching agreements that take account of fairness and ability to pay while maintaining overall a cost-effective approach. The EU Member States are, after all, a grouping of developed countries that are remarkably diverse in terms of economic profile and energy mix.

TABLE 4.1 National targets for 2020 for the non-ETS sectors

	% change in 2020 compared to 2005	Allocation ($MtCO_2$)	
		2013	2020
Belgium	−15	81.2	70.2
Bulgaria	20	27.3	28.8
Czech Republic	9	63.6	86.3
Denmark	−20	35.9	29.7
Germany	−14	487.1	437.6
Estonia	−14	6.1	6.3
Ireland	−20	45.2	37.5
Greece	−4	58.9	60.7
Spain	−10	228.9	215.5
France	−14	397.9	363.1
Croatia	11	20.6	21.8
Italy	−13	310.1	296.3
Cyprus	−5	5.6	5.5
Latvia	17	9.0	9.6
Lithuania	15	16.7	18.6
Luxembourg	−20	9.7	8.3
Hungary	10	49.3	57.0
Malta	5	1.1	1.1
Netherlands	−16	121.8	106.4
Austria	−16	54.0	49.6
Poland	−16	197.9	204.6
Portugal	1	47.6	49.5
Romania	19	79.1	90.1
Slovenia	4	11.9	12.1
Slovakia	13	25.0	27.3
Finland	−16	32.7	29.2
Sweden	−17	42.5	37.9
United Kingdom	−16	350.0	319.8
EU-28		2,816.5	2,679.9

Source: Commission Decision 2013/162/EU of 26 March 2013 on determining Member States' annual emission allocations (2013–2020) pursuant to Decision No. 406/2009/EC of the European Parliament and of the Council, OJ L 90, 28.3.2013, pp. 106–110.

Conclusion: the emission reductions for sectors outside the EU ETS have been shared out between Member States in a way that reflects their differences in GDP *per capita*. Through flexibilities in implementation, an overall cost-effective result can be maintained.

Controlling non-CO_2 greenhouse gases

Non-CO_2 greenhouse gases (methane, nitrous oxides and fluorinated gases or F-gases) made up 27% of the EU's greenhouse gas emissions in 1990 (see Table 4.2). By 2010 their share had decreased to around 22%. This reduction is faster than the overall reduction in greenhouse gas emissions of 15% in the same period. The reduction in methane and nitrous oxides emissions is particularly pronounced but is partially compensated by a sharp increase in the use of F-gases (i.e. HFCs, but also PFCs and SF_6). These reductions have been brought about as a secondary benefit from several pieces of environmental legislation.

The reduction in methane emissions is partially related to developments in the agricultural sector. For example, quotas for milk production existed until recently under EU agriculture policy. These quotas combined with productivity gains limited emissions. As part of the reform of the EU's Common Agricultural Policy (CAP) a ban on stubble burning was agreed in order to maintain soil organic matter.[3] This ban may reduce methane emissions from

TABLE 4.2 Development of non-CO_2 emissions in relation to CO_2 emissions in the EU

	1990	1995	2000	2005	2010	2012
CO_2 without LULUCF	4,437	4,149	4,136	4,262	3,908	3,401
CH_4 (methane)	607	552	501	449	413	403
N_2O (nitrous oxide)	533	474	417	402	350	341
HFCs	28	41	47	62	82	86
PFCs	21	14	10	6	3	3
SF_6	11	16	11	7	6	6
Sum without LULUCF	5,626	5,253	5,122	5,178	4,751	4,544

Sources: Annual European Union greenhouse gas inventory 1990–2010 and inventory report 2012; Technical report No. 3/2012. European Environment Agency, Copenhagen.

agriculture by 0.5% in 2030 (up to some 1 million tonnes of CO_2-equivalent (MtCO_2eq) per year).

Methane emissions from the waste sector fell by 35% between 1990 and 2010, mainly as a result of the EU Landfill Directive.[4] The Directive requires biodegradable waste to be diverted from landfills to reduce the volume of biodegradable waste that is landfilled by 65% in 2018. Several Member States, such as Austria, Belgium, Denmark, Germany and the Netherlands, have even banned the landfilling of biodegradable waste. The EU's forthcoming policy initiatives on resource efficiency and the 'circular economy' are expected to further reduce methane emissions.

Between 2011 and 2013, the European Commission carried out a comprehensive review of the EU's existing air quality policy which showed to have had significant benefits in terms of reducing greenhouse gas emissions. In December 2013, A 'Clean Air Programme for Europe' was tabled[5] with new air quality objectives for the period up to 2030, with stricter national emission ceilings for six main pollutants, including methane. Methane emissions not only act as a greenhouse gas but also increase ground-level ozone (summer smog) in the EU. The methane ceilings of the Clean Air Programme are based on measures that are expected to be implemented at low cost.[6] Costs can even be negative if the revenues from the methane captured (for example, from anaerobic digestion) are higher than the costs of distributing and using the gas. The national ceilings are Member State specific. The proposal would require reductions in methane between 7% and 55% in 2030 compared to 2005. For the EU as whole a reduction of 33% is proposed for 2030 but targets are also proposed for individual Member States. As of April 2015 the proposal was still being negotiated with EU Member States and the European Parliament.

The EU Nitrates Directive[7] has reduced animal manure spreading and mineral fertiliser use over time. Indirectly, this has reduced emissions of nitrous oxide (N_2O) from agriculture. The emissions of nitrous oxide from the production of nitric acid, adipic acid and glyoxal and glyoxal acid are also regulated by the inclusion of these sectors in the EU ETS as of 2013.

Fluorinated gases, or F-gases as they are often known, are very powerful greenhouse gases. Their potential warming effect on the atmosphere can be up to 23,000 times higher than carbon dioxide. These gases are used for example in refrigerators, air conditioning, foams, and heat pumps, as aerosols or in fire protection. The EU has banned certain uses of hydro fluorocarbons (HFCs) and other fluorinated greenhouse gases. It has put in place strict rules to prevent leakage from products and to ensure appropriate treatment at the end of their life.[8] These measures were taken in response to the sharp increase in the use of HFCs as the main alternative for ozone depleting substances that were no longer allowed under the Montreal Protocol. One of the paradoxes of the Montreal Protocol was that substances, such as HFCs, solved the problem of protecting the ozone layer but had the unintentional side effect of being very potent greenhouse gases.

The EU Mobile Air Conditioning (MAC)[9] Directive requires that all new passenger cars sold from 1 January 2011 have to use cooling agents with a greenhouse warming potential of fewer than 150 times that of CO_2. From 2018, all new passenger cars have to use more climate friendly refrigerants in their air conditioning systems. The EU Directive on proper handling of end-of-life vehicles[10] has required the collection and proper disposal of scrapped mobile air conditioners.

Perfluorocarbons (PFCs) released from primary aluminium production are covered by the EU ETS Directive (from 2013 onwards). The small number of producers in the semiconductor industry that emit PFCs made a Voluntary Agreement to reduce their PFC emissions by 10% in 2010 compared to 1995, and in fact the industry achieved a 41% absolute reduction in this period.[11]

With the help of all the above measures, F-gases have ceased to increase further but have stabilised at levels of 110 to 120 $MtCO_2$eq. This is still, however, a level inconsistent with a 40% greenhouse gas reduction foreseen for 2030. In 2014, therefore, a new F-gas Regulation[12] was adopted to phase down the total amount of HFCs that can be sold in the EU from 2015 to one fifth of today's sales by 2030. This is expected to cut emissions by around 70 $MtCO_2$eq in 2030 at marginal costs per tonne roughly equal to the overall marginal costs needed to reduce the EU's greenhouse gas emissions by 40% in 2030. By 2030 the Regulation is expected to reduce the EU's F-gas emissions by two thirds compared to today's levels (see Figure 4.2).

The measure is a landmark piece of legislation in that it stimulates innovation while allowing European companies to keep their leadership in the sector. It is hoped that the Regulation should facilitate a global agreement on the global phase-down of the consumption and production of HFCs under the Montreal Protocol.

Conclusion: several regulations in the field of environment and agriculture have had a beneficial impact on the EU's greenhouse gas emissions, in particular as regards methane. On the very potent fluorinated gases, specific legislation has been put in place that has stimulated EU technological leadership worldwide.

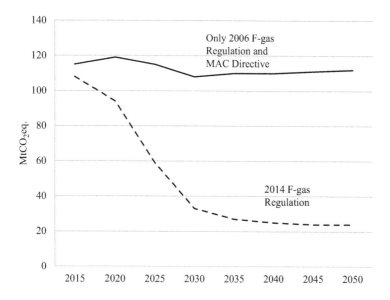

FIGURE 4.2 Expected impact of the new F-gas Regulation on EU HFC emissions (in $MtCO_2eq$)

Land use, land-use change and forestry

Agricultural land and forests cover more than three quarters of EU territory, and hold large stocks of carbon, preventing its release into the atmosphere. Today's forests and soils (i.e. those existing since 1990) are the biggest store of carbon in the EU. Moreover the store is increasing each year. This makes them important for climate policy. Deforestation or changing grassland into cropland risks decreasing the amount of carbon stored. Afforestation and improved land and forest management might, on the other hand, increase the amount of carbon stored. These modifications in the use of land have been termed in the UNFCCC jargon as 'LULUCF', standing for 'Land Use, Land-Use Change and Forestry'.

The LULUCF sector has been a net carbon sink in the EU. In the period 1990 to 2012 an amount of carbon of around 250 to 320 $MtCO_2$ per year was stored (see Figure 4.3). This amounts to between 5% to 10% of the EU's greenhouse gas emissions (EEA, 2014: 1203). Figure 4.3 indicates that the LULUCF sink has remained more or less constant over the period. However, projections suggest that with increasing demand for timber and biomass, combined with ageing forests, the LULUCF sink in the EU may decline (Capros et al., 2014: 59). This depends, however, on a number of factors, such as how forests are managed, the extent to which timber and biomass demand increases, how much biomass is imported, and the type and source of biomass supplied (whether forest, agriculture or plantation biomass).

The actions of farmers and forest owners that store carbon in forests and soils have only been partially recognised in climate policy, if at all. If farmers and foresters store more carbon, the negative effects of climate change are being limited. However, this potential positive contribution is not fully valued: direct economic incentives to store carbon are largely absent or, at best, incomplete. This is also due to difficulties of collecting robust carbon data with respect to forests and soils.

Changes in the carbon stored by the EU's LULUCF sector are not counted towards the 20% greenhouse gas reduction target in 2020. Only a minority of EU Member States engage in the monitoring, reporting and verification of cropland and grassland emissions. A major reason for this is the large uncertainty in the estimates. Whereas emissions of energy CO_2 can be estimated with an accuracy of 1% or 2%, estimates of the amount of carbon stored in soils, crops and forests have a range of uncertainty which is significantly higher. All other things being equal, the reduction achieved by a power plant is considered more certain than the tonne estimated to have been reduced by the forest. The amount stored in the forest is also influenced

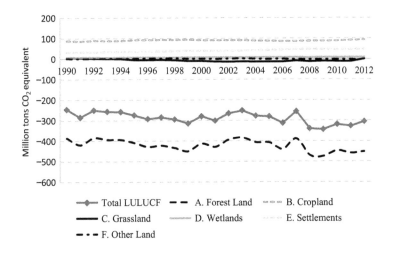

FIGURE 4.3 LULUCF emissions in the EU-28
Source: EEA.

by sun, wind, fires and rain. Also the co-benefits of mitigation measures are not easily comparable: air quality benefits due to a more efficient power plant may be easier to estimate than the benefits of improved biodiversity or water management of forest conservation.

Although LULUCF emissions were therefore excluded from the EU's internal 20% greenhouse gas reduction target in 2020, their measurement, and to a certain degree their contribution, has become part of the EU's Kyoto Protocol obligations, with mandatory accounting for forestry (afforestation, deforestation and forest management) but voluntary inclusion of grassland and cropland management. In addition, LULUCF emissions are affected by the way the 20% greenhouse gases are reduced in the EU. If this reduction would rely, for example, on a large increase in the use of biomass in the energy sector, this could lead to a reduction in the amount of carbon stored in the forest. Projections available at the end of 2013 indicate that the LULUCF sink for the 28 EU Member States might decrease (perhaps by some 10%) by 2030 compared to 2005 (Capros et al., 2014: 59–63). This is a result of an expected increase in the demand for timber, including demand for biomass for energy. One should note, however, that there are many modelling uncertainties that qualify such estimates.

In order to reduce the uncertainties in the data and to improve the scope of the sources covered, the EU adopted in 2013 a decision on accounting rules on greenhouse gas emissions and removals related to LULUCF.[13] These accounting rules are consistent with agreements made during the UNFCCC negotiations on the second commitment period of the Kyoto Protocol.[14] Furthermore, Member States are now obliged to adopt action plans that provide information on LULUCF actions to limit or reduce emissions and to maintain or increase removals of carbon. However, the sector still does not have a specific greenhouse gas target under EU regulations.

For the period 2013 to 2020, all Member States have to account for emissions and removals from afforestation, reforestation, deforestation and forest management. The same applies for producing emissions estimates from cropland and grazing land management, for which annual accounting also becomes mandatory as of 2021. Re-vegetation and wetlands are accounted for on a voluntary basis following specific rules. The accounting shall include the following carbon stocks: above and below ground biomass, litter, dead wood, soil organic carbon and harvested wood products. Notably, the amount of carbon stored in wood products (sawn wood, wood panels and paper) has also to be taken into account. This is in view of the fact that the carbon is not released immediately into the atmosphere, but is stored in products such as furniture and building structures for a certain period.

More specifically, accounting for afforestation, reforestation and deforestation must reflect emission and removals on lands that were not forests on 31 December 1989 (hence from 1990 onwards). For management of forests that existed before 1 January 1990, removals are calculated compared to a reference projection for the commitment period, taking into account a number of factors, such as the age of the forest, standard management practice and natural circumstances (forest fires and storms, for example) that can lead to large variations between the years. The reference level gives an estimate of the expected annual net emissions (or net removals) from forest management for the period 2013–2020 without climate policies in place. If more CO_2 is removed from the atmosphere than compared to this reference level in an accounting period (e.g. 2013–2020 this counts as removals in the LULUCF account under the Kyoto Protocol). However, the use of forest management emissions and removals for compliance with the Kyoto Protocol is limited to 3.5% of the Member State's total greenhouse gas emissions of its base year under the Kyoto Protocol.[15]

The use of the forest management reference levels creates an incentive for EU Member States, and other Parties to the Kyoto Protocol, to conserve the carbon stored in existing forests by, for example, changing the way forests are managed (such as by selective logging as opposed to clear-cutting). Table 4.3 gives an overview of the agreed forest management reference levels for the EU Member States. The size of the number gives an indication of the relevance of the forest sector in the country. Strikingly, more than 70% of the carbon stored in (existing) managed forest in the EU is stored in only seven Member States.

The 2013 Decision has to be seen as an important first step towards the inclusion of the LULUCF sector in the EU's emission reduction commitment itself. It aims to reduce uncertainties and ensure full coverage of Member States' reporting and accounting of LULUCF sectors. This in turn provides the required data and tools for subsequent improvements to these reporting and accounting rules.

As part of its 2030 climate and energy policy framework, the Commission has proposed to also look into a more holistic approach to the land-use sector[16] which would include the LULUCF sector in the EU's climate target but in a manner that ensures that synergies can be found across sectors. Currently, the same piece of land is affected by various pieces of climate-relevant legislation. Carbon stored in agricultural soils (such as grassland) is not yet accounted for towards the EU's 2020 targets whereas methane emissions from cows grazing on the same grassland are counted (as part of the Effort Sharing Decision). Turning cropland into grassland might increase methane

TABLE 4.3 Forest management reference levels, 2013–20, for the EU-28

Country	Kton CO$_2$eq.	Country	Kton CO$_2$eq.
Austria	–6,516	Latvia	–16,302
Belgium	–2,499	Lithuania	–4,552
Bulgaria	–7,950	Luxembourg	–418
Cyprus	–157	Malta	–49
Czech Republic	–4,686	Netherlands	–1,425
Denmark	409	Poland	–2,7133
Estonia	–2,741	Portugal	–6,830
Finland	–20,466	Romania	–15,793
France	–67,140	Slovakia	–1,084
Germany	–22,148	Slovenia	–3,171
Greece	–1,830	Spain	– 23,100
Hungary	4.3	Sweden	–41,336
Ireland	–142	United Kingdom	–8,268
Italy	–22,166	Croatia	–6,289
EU-28	–31,3025		

Sources: For EU-27: Annex II to Decision No. 529/2013/EU, and for Croatia: Appendix to FCCC/KP/CMP/2011/10/Add.1.
Note: Most Member States take account of the carbon stored in harvest wood products except Croatia, Greece, Luxembourg and Malta.

emissions (if increasing the number of cattle) but may also store more carbon in the soil. At present, increasing the use of biomass in the energy sector leads to reductions of emissions under the ETS or Effort Sharing Decision while there may be no incentive to avoid increased emissions or reduced absorption under the LULUCF sector. Therefore the inclusion of LULUCF into the EU should ensure for a more coherent approach across sectors to reduce emissions.

For those reasons the EU's Heads of State and Government decided in October 2014 to include agriculture and forestry into the overall target of 'at least 40%' reduction by 2030. Such an approach could, for example, build on the existing Effort Sharing Decision governing the non-EU ETS sectors (by including LULUCF), or could construct an explicit separate (third) land-use pillar (in addition to the EU ETS and the Effort Sharing Decision sectors), or a combination of both. Clearly, the promotion of cost-efficiency and environmental integrity has to be at the forefront of these considerations. Further analysis is needed to assess the mitigation potential and the most appropriate policy approach.

Conclusion: carbon emissions from land use, land-use change and forestry are not covered by the EU's 2020 targets, but complete emission inventories are being established. It has been decided that these sinks are to be an integral part of the climate and energy framework for 2030, but the modalities are still being elaborated.

Adaptation and the mainstreaming of climate action

Another EU policy area that frames national and domestic policies concerns the field of adaptation to climate change. In comparison to mitigation, the EU was late in formulating its own adaptation policy. However in 2013 the Commission presented a comprehensive strategy on adaptation[17] in order to make Europe more climate resilient. Extreme weather events have indeed been intensifying over the last decades, whether it is increased flooding, heat waves or water restrictions. Climate change manifests itself at the local level, and hence the EU policy has basically been about encouraging Member States to develop their own climate adaptation plans.

The impacts of climate change are very diverse across the EU. In mountainous regions, such as the Alps or the Pyrenees, glaciers are melting at a much faster pace; many have already entirely disappeared. In the North there is the Arctic region, where the changes are probably the most pronounced as the permanent ice retreats much faster. The Arctic region is undergoing profound natural changes leading also to increased geopolitical attention, ranging from the exploration of underground resources that were not previously accessible to the opening of new navigation routes. The Mediterranean area is confronted with increased water stress, and desertification in some areas. The North West of Europe needs to prepare for a higher sea level, as many areas, big cities and major industrial zones are close to the sea and situated in low-lying areas.

The EU Adaptation strategy encourages Member States to develop their adaptation plans with their neighbours, in particular in view of undertaking transboundary action. Special focus is put on urban areas, which are often ill equipped, and a stream of action has been developed as part of the successful Covenant of the Mayors' initiative. Another major focus of attention is making infrastructure in the field of transport, energy and construction more climate resilient. European standardisation bodies are involved in this work. A third work stream is to engage with insurance providers to urge the creation of insurance products that offer increased protection to consumers against the effects of climate change.

At EU level two specific actions have been developed, one on finance and one on knowledge-sharing. The EU Adaptation strategy recognises that improved access to funding will be critical in building a climate-resilient Europe. One third of the EU budget is spent on regional aid through the so-called Structural and Investment Funds. Adaptation, along with mitigation, is being mainstreamed into regional policies, and into other areas of EU spending, such that a political commitment has been agreed to spend at least 20% of the EU budget on actions that have a direct and indirect link to climate change.[18] Furthermore, a tracking system for EU budget expenditure has been put in place to guarantee this objective is met. This is particularly important as these funds flow predominantly to those Member States and regions that are less wealthy than the EU average. Through the EU's budgetary spending, there is clear evidence of solidarity and the wish for fairness in the field of climate action.

The EU is also investing in knowledge-sharing and best practice. Adaptation to climate change manifests itself in unique ways at the local level, but experiences can nevertheless be very similar. In particular in developing adaptation policies a wealth of success stories exist at the local level. Therefore a web-based European platform has been created called 'Climate-ADAPT' (see http://climate-adapt.eea.europa.eu), which is designed to help Europe adapt to climate change by the sharing of information and best practice. This has effectively become a one-stop-shop for adaptation information in Europe. Furthermore, in order to encourage adaptation policy experimentation, grants of limited size are available through a dedicated climate change sub-programme of the LIFE fund within the EU budget.

Conclusion: the EU has developed an adaptation strategy that encourages and assists Member States in developing adaptation plans and policies. At EU level, the mainstreaming of adaptation and mitigation is reflected through a commitment to spend at least 20% of EU funds on climate-related expenditure through to 2020. Cooperation exists with the Covenant of the Mayors' initiative and information sharing happens through the Climate-ADAPT web-based platform.

Notes

1 Decision No. 406/2009/EC of the European Parliament and of the Council of 23 April 2009 on the effort of Member States to reduce their greenhouse gas emissions to meet the Community's greenhouse gas emission reduction commitments up to 2020; OJ L 140, 5.6.2009, pp. 136-148: http://eur-lex.europa.eu/LexUriServ/LexUriServ.do?uri=OJ:L:2009:140:0136:0148:EN:PDF

2 Commission Decision 2013/162/EU of 26 March 2013 on determining Member States' annual emission allocations for the period from 2013 to 2020 pursuant to Decision No. 406/2009/EC of the European Parliament and of the Council; OJ L 90, 28.3.2013, pp. 106-110: http://eur-lex.europa.eu/legal-content/EN/TXT/PDF/?uri=CELEX:32013D0162&from=EN. Figures based on the greenhouse gas warming potentials of the IPCC Second Assessment Report.

3 Regulation No. 1306/2013 of the European Parliament and of the Council of 17 December 2013 on the financing, management and monitoring of the common agricultural policy and repealing Council Regulations (EEC) No. 352/78, (EC) No. 165/94, (EC) No. 2799/98, (EC) No. 814/2000, (EC) No. 1290/2005 and (EC) No. 485/2008 Annex II. Rules on cross compliance to Article 93, OJ, L 347/602/603, 20.12.2013.

4 Council Directive 1999/31/EC of 26 April 1999 on the landfill of waste; OJ L 182, 16.7.1999, pp. 1-19: http://eur-lex.europa.eu/legal-content/EN/TXT/PDF/?uri=CELEX:31999L0031&from=en

5 For all documents related to the Clean Air Policy Package, see: http://ec.europa.eu/environment/air/clean_air_policy.htm

6 Proposal for a Directive of the European Parliament and of the Council on the reduction of national emissions of certain atmospheric pollutants and amending Directive 2003/35/EC, COM(2013) 920 final of 18.12.2013: http://eur-lex.europa.eu/resource.html?uri=cellar:5fbb1091-77a9-11e3-b889-01aa75ed71a1.0021.04/DOC_1&format=PDF (Annexes to the Proposal available at: http://eur-lex.europa.eu/resource.html?uri=cellar:5fbb1091-77a9-11e3-b889-01aa75ed71a1.0021.04/DOC_2&format=PDF).

7 Council Directive of 12 December 1991 concerning the protection of waters against pollution caused by nitrates from agricultural sources; OJ L 375, 31.12.1991, pp. 1-8: http://eur-lex.europa.eu/legal-content/EN/TXT/PDF/?uri=CELEX:31991L0676&from=fr

8 Regulation (EC) No. 842/2006 of the European Parliament and of the Council of 17 May 2006 on certain fluorinated greenhouse gases; OJ L 161, 14.6.2006, pp. 1-11: http://eur-lex.europa.eu/legal-content/EN/TXT/PDF/?uri=CELEX:32006R0842&from=EN

9 Directive 2006/40/EC of the European Parliament and of the Council of 17 May 2006 relating to emissions from air-conditioning systems in motor vehicles and amending Council Directive 70/156/EEC; OJ L 161, 14.6.2006, pp. 12-18: http://eur-lex.europa.eu/legal-content/EN/TXT/PDF/?uri=CELEX:32006L0040&from=EN

10 Directive 2000/53/EC of the European Parliament and of the Council of 18 September 2000 on end-of-life vehicles; OJ L 269, 21.10.2000, pp. 34-43:

http://eur-lex.europa.eu/resource.html?uri=cellar:02fa83cf-bf28-4afc-8f9f-eb201bd61813.0005.02/DOC_1&format=PDF

11 www.eeca.eu/esia/public-policy/sustainability-esh/pfc-gases

12 Regulation (EU) No. 517/2014 of the European Parliament and of the Council of 16 April 2014 on fluorinated greenhouse gases and repealing Regulation (EC) No. 842/2006; OJ L 150, 20.5.2014, pp. 195-230: http://eur-lex.europa.eu/legal-content/EN/TXT/PDF/?uri=CELEX:32014R0517&from=EN

13 Decision No. 529/2013/EU of the European Parliament and of the Council of 21 May 2013 on accounting rules on greenhouse gas emissions and removals resulting from activities relating to land use, land-use change and forestry and on information concerning actions relating to those activities; OJ L 165, 18.6.2013, pp. 80-97: http://eur-lex.europa.eu/legal-content/EN/TXT/PDF/?uri=CELEX:32013D0529&from=EN

14 Definitions, modalities, rules and guidelines relating to land use, land-use change and forestry activities under the Kyoto Protocol (FCCC/KP/CMP/2011/10/Add.1), 15 March 2012: http://unfccc.int/resource/docs/2011/cmp7/eng/10a01.pdf

15 Decision No. 529/2013/EU of the European Parliament and of the Council of 21 May 2013: Recital 12: 'The accounting rules should provide for an upper limit applicable to net removals for forest management that may be entered into accounts.' Article 6(2) says: 'Member States shall include in their forest management accounts total emissions and removals of no more than the equivalent of 3.5 per cent of a Member State's emissions in its base year.'

16 European Commission (2014) A policy framework for climate and energy in the period from 2020 to 2030. COM(2014) 15 final of 22.1.2014: http://eur-lex.europa.eu/legal-content/EN/TXT/PDF/?uri=CELEX:52014DC0015&from=EN

17 European Commission (2013) 'An EU Strategy on adaptation to climate change', COM(2013) 216 final dated 16.4.2013: http://eur-lex.europa.eu/legal-content/EN/TXT/PDF/?uri=CELEX:52013DC0216&from=EN

18 European Council Conclusions (EUCO 37/13) of 8 February 2013, Paragraph 10: 'The optimal achievement of objectives in some policy areas depends on the mainstreaming of priorities such as environmental protection into a range of instruments in other policy areas. Climate action objectives will represent at least 20% of EU spending in the period 2014-2020 and therefore be reflected in the appropriate instruments to ensure that they contribute to strengthen energy security, building a low-carbon, resource efficient and climate resilient economy that will enhance Europe's competitiveness and create more and greener jobs.' (Document consulted 10.4.2015: www.consilium.europa.eu/uedocs/cms_data/docs/pressdata/en/ec/135344.pdf)

References

Capros, P., Matzos, L., Parousos, L., Tasios, N., Klaassen, G., and van Ierland, T. (2011) 'Analysis of the EU policy package on climate change and renewables' *Energy Policy* 39: 476–1485.

Capros, P., de Vita, A., Tasios, N., Papadopoulos, D., Siskos, P., Apostolaki, E., Zampara, M., Paroussos, L., Fragiadakis, K., Kouvaritakis, N., Hoglund-Isaksson, L., Winiwarter, W., Purohit, P., Böttcher, H., Frank, S., Havlik, P., Gusti M., and Witzke, H.P. (2014) *EU energy, transport and GHG emissions: trends to 2050, reference scenario 2013*, Luxembourg: Publications office of the European Union (http://ec.europa.eu/clima/policies/2030/models/eu_trends_2050_en.pdf).

Delbeke, J., G. Klaassen, T. van Ierland and P. Zapfel (2010) 'The Role of Environmental Economics in Recent Policy Making at the European Commission' *Review of Environmental Economics and Policy* 4:24–43.

EEA (2014) *Annual European Union greenhouse gas inventory 1990–2012 and inventory report 2014, Technical report Submission to the UNFCCC Secretariat*; EEA Technical report No. 9/2014, European Environment Agency, Copenhagen, p. 1203.

Tol, R. (2009) 'Intra-union flexibility of non-ETS emission reduction obligations in the European Union' *Energy Policy* 37:1745–1752.

5

THE EU AND INTERNATIONAL CLIMATE CHANGE POLICY

Jake Werksman, Jürgen Lefevere and Artur Runge-Metzger

Introduction

Since the 1990s, the EU has played a leading role in the development of international climate change policy. International climate change policy has, over the past twenty years, shaped the EU's domestic climate change policy. This dynamic of leadership and learning reflects the EU's strong commitment to a multilateral response to climate change. It also reflects the EU's understanding that it cannot successfully combat climate change on its own. It is therefore necessary to encourage others and build partnerships with other countries. Ambitious European climate policy will increasingly depend upon the rest of the world acting collectively, and with comparable ambition, to reduce greenhouse gas emissions.

This chapter describes the stages in the development of international climate change policy, from the 1992 United Nations Framework Convention on Climate Change (UNFCCC), via the 1997 Kyoto Protocol, to the current negotiations on a new agreement to be reached in Paris in 2015 (2015 Agreement). Throughout these negotiations, the EU has, together with other progressive countries, called for international agreements that are: (1) ambitious and inclusive, by ensuring that all countries play a role in reducing greenhouse gas emissions in line with what science indicates is necessary; (2) fair, by taking into account the common but different responsibilities, capabilities and vulnerabilities of countries at different levels of economic development; and (3) robust, by providing a strong legal basis for holding all countries accountable for the commitments that they make.

As will be described, the international community has not yet been able to reach an agreement that is sufficiently ambitious and inclusive, fair, and robust to have the potential to reduce global emissions to levels scientists would consider safe. But international climate policy, like EU climate policy, has made important, incremental progress, and two decades of experience has yielded critical lessons for future action. As the negotiations proceed towards the 2015 Agreement, which will determine international climate policy from 2020 onwards, the EU is working with its partners to ensure these lessons are applied.

The 2015 Agreement will need to take into account major structural changes in the global economy since 1992, by covering emissions from all major economies. It will, however, need to be sensitive to the fact that many countries are beginning to regulate greenhouse gases for the first time. Thus, the 2015 Agreement will need to allow for a wide diversity of commitments that reflect significant differences in countries' starting points. This diversity will need to be brought together under a common framework of rules for reporting on emissions that will enable governments and the public to track performance over time.

While designing the 2015 Agreement, it must be recognised that there are limits to the role that a multilateral agreement – involving more than 190 countries – can play in setting common standards for specific national and regional policies, such as the use of carbon markets. In that respect it will be different from the Kyoto Protocol, which was created at a time when there were no national or regional carbon markets and climate policies generally were only in their infancy. Meeting the Protocol's targets gave the initial impetus for the EU's carbon market, but the Protocol has since failed to keep up with the learning and further development of domestic and regional markets. The 2015 Agreement will need to enable the further development of national and regional climate policies, while at the same time encourage their ambition, effectiveness and transparency.

The 2015 Agreement cannot focus on cutting emissions alone. It will need to respond to the needs of the poorest countries, which will continue to require financial and technical support to transition towards a low-carbon future. Countries vulnerable to the impacts of climate change will need support in building resilience to higher temperatures, rising seas and extremes in weather. Finally, the outcome in Paris will need to acknowledge that legally binding agreements between governments can only provide part of the solution. In order to transform a fossil fuel-based economy into a low-carbon economy, the tens of billions of public sector finance and development assistance made available by governments will need to leverage trillions in commercial investments. Governments, of both developed and developing countries, need to learn how to better recognise and incentivise actions by cities, local authorities and the private sector.

> Conclusion: the international community has not yet been able to reach an agreement that is sufficiently ambitious and inclusive, fair and robust to reduce global emissions to levels scientists would consider safe. The Kyoto Protocol helped the EU to shape its domestic policies, such as the carbon market. The 2015 Agreement should, in a similar manner, act as a catalyst to the development of domestic policies in all countries.

A brief history of the UNFCCC

The 1992 UNFCCC is a framework treaty with 195 Parties – a near universal membership of States. The UNFCCC sets a long-term, science-based objective which calls for the stabilisation of greenhouse gas concentrations in the atmosphere at safe levels. The Parties have since clarified that this will mean limiting global average temperature rise to less than 2°C as compared to pre-industrial levels. The UNFCCC also sets out principles and establishes bodies and procedures to guide future international negotiations towards this objective.

The UNFCCC has succeeded in ensuring that climate change remains an important issue near the top of the international policy agenda. Its annual Conferences of the Parties (COPs) regularly attract the participation of more than 100 ministers and many Heads of State. It demands better data and analysis, spurring support for the development of climate science, both domestically and internationally. Its reporting requirements and capacity-building programmes have ensured that most countries now regularly collect and report on greenhouse gas emissions from their economies.

The financial and market-based mechanisms established under the UNFCCC have channelled billions of euros of investment in mitigation and adaptation in developing countries, through new financial institutions and through market-based mechanisms that have expanded and tested the boundaries of what is possible through international cooperation. The EU and its Member States have played a major role in this success, as world's largest provider of development finance, and the world's largest carbon market.

However, the UNFCCC process has struggled to reach agreement on specific emission reduction targets that are ambitious and inclusive enough to put the world on track not to exceed the below-2°C objective. In the early 1990s, when the Framework Convention on Climate Change was being negotiated, a scientific and political consensus on the risks of climate change was still emerging. Many actors perceived efforts to reduce greenhouse gas emissions to be primarily the concern and responsibility of wealthy industrialised nations. These countries are historically the largest emitters of greenhouse gases, with the resources to invest in alternative technologies. Developing countries could only be expected to take action on climate change if it were consistent with their overriding responsibilities to reduce poverty and promote economic growth.

In order to achieve the broad political consensus necessary to adopt the Convention, negotiators recognised that developed and developing countries had 'common but differentiated responsibilities and respective capabilities', a principle that led to the design of a treaty that divided Parties into 'developed' (Annex I) countries (members, in 1992, of the Organisation for Economic Co-operation and Development, Eastern European countries and the Former Soviet Union); and 'developing' country Parties (the rest of the world).

While all UNFCCC Parties are expected to put in place and report on policies to mitigate and adapt to climate change, Annex I countries took on an additional, if softly worded, commitment to aim to stabilise their greenhouse gas emissions at 1990 levels by the year 2000. The richest of the Annex I countries (OECD members listed in Annex II) were also required to provide an unspecified level of 'new and additional' financial support to developing countries that chose to take action on climate change.

This division of responsibilities between developed and developing countries, based on their development status in 1992, often referred to as 'the firewall', continues to shape climate politics.

The UNFCCC, therefore, provided an important first basis for international climate policy. Among the most important of the Convention's commitments is the collective procedural obligation to review the adequacy of Parties' commitments to mitigate greenhouse gas emissions 'in light of the best available scientific information' on climate change and to 'take appropriate action' including through the adoption of additional Protocols or amendments to the Convention. The first major effort at better aligning Parties' mitigation commitments with the Convention's objective concluded with the adoption of the Kyoto Protocol in 1997.

While the Kyoto Protocol was designed to set the world on a low-carbon pathway by capping and reducing the emissions of industrialised countries between 2008 and 2012, it was severely undermined by the decision in 2001 by the US – then the world's largest emitter of greenhouse gases – not to ratify the Kyoto Protocol. While the US has in the past decades developed a reputation for failing to ratify international treaties that it has helped to design, the US's fundamental objection to the Kyoto Protocol was its perpetuation of the UNFCCC 'firewall' by setting targets and timetables exclusively for Annex I (developed country) Parties.

Since then, the international community has struggled with attempts to strengthen and expand the scope of the Kyoto Protocol, and/or to design an ambitious new agreement that could secure the meaningful participation of the US, as well as emerging economies whose emissions have been growing rapidly.

The most recent effort to negotiate a new agreement that would replace the Kyoto Protocol and engage the US, the rest of the industrialised world and the emerging economies, failed, at the 2009 Climate Summit in Copenhagen. Instead of delivering a new, legally binding treaty that many (including the EU) had hoped for, these negotiations led to the informal Copenhagen Accords, reflected formally a year later in the Cancun Agreement. An international registry of domestic climate mitigation policies was set up, whereby each country notifies its pledge unilaterally and without international discussion or negotiation.

The unilateral, or 'bottom-up', nature of the Copenhagen–Cancun pledging process allowed for a more inclusive international approach. For the first time the US, China, India, Brazil, South Africa, the EU and many middle- and low-income countries made pledges at the international level to achieve specific domestic climate policies as part of this initiative.

However, in addition to being voluntary, a number of the pledges made by major economies are conditioned, for example on others taking more ambitious action and the availability of financial resources. Most importantly, current pledges leave a substantial 'ambition gap': even if fully implemented, these pledges would lead to a temperature rise of 3.5°C instead of the maximum 2°C that is recommended by scientists.

Conclusion: the Kyoto Protocol was signed but not ratified by the US. An attempt to adopt a similar agreement failed in Copenhagen in 2009. Since then a 'bottom-up' pledging process led to some progress but has not delivered the emission reductions necessary to respect the below-2°C objective.

A fundamental change in the landscape

The fundamental challenge revealed by these two efforts is how to limit global emissions of greenhouse gases consistent with the UNFCCC objective while allocating those limits among countries in a way that is broadly perceived as fair. The science tells us that the world has to peak its emissions by 2020, reduce by 50% by 2050, and reach near zero levels by the end of the present century. Using the 1992 division of developed (Annex I) and developing (non-Annex I) countries, it is possible to map out emissions pathways that would require Annex I reductions in the order of 85% by 2050, beginning now and delivering a 30% reduction by 2020. In the meantime, non-Annex I emissions could continue to grow until 2020, and decline thereafter at a similar trajectory as Annex I countries (see Figure 5.1).

However, since 1992, the world has not followed this path. As indicated in Figure 5.2 Annex I country emissions have plateaued but do not yet show signs, as a group, of a steep decline. The most spectacular change is undoubtedly the industrialisation and rising emissions of China which is now by far the largest emitter with more than 12 billion tonnes per year, twice as much as the US and three times as much as the EU.

Behind this spectacular change, more noteworthy evolutions took place. Chinese per capita emissions are now higher than the EU's. And while India

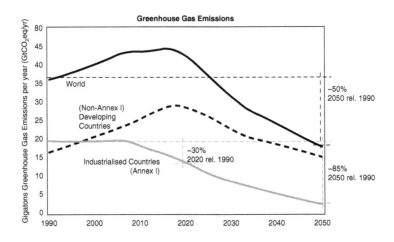

FIGURE 5.1 A possible pathway to the below-2°C objective

Sources: European Commission, adapted from original data provided by JRC, PBL and IIASA.

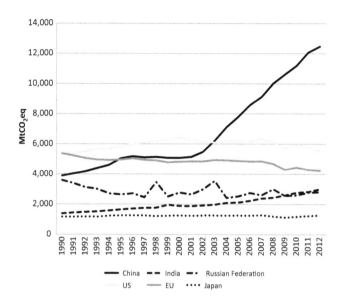

FIGURE 5.2 Emissions of major economies, 1990–2012 (all greenhouse gases, all sources and sinks)

Sources: historical emissions data: inventories data to the UNFCCC (http://unfccc.int/national_reports), emissions with Land Use, Land-Use Change and Forestry; for China and India data from EDGAR, all greenhouse gas emissions, all sources and sinks, excl. forest and peat fires.

is now the world's third largest emitter of greenhouse gases, persistent poverty has kept its per capita emissions relatively low (Figure 5.3). Any future international climate change agreement will need to recalibrate the UNFCCC principle of 'common but differentiated responsibilities and respective capabilities' to align with this new reality, and accelerate the plateauing and reduction of emissions across all major economies.

Another noteworthy structural change is the emissions intensity of economic development over the same period. Measured per unit of GDP, emissions have been going down significantly in all parts of the world, industrialised as well as emerging economies. Figure 5.4 gives an overview and offers some hope that the trend that was observed in the EU since 1990, of growing GDP and declining emissions, may become closer to reality for the world as a whole. The fact that emissions in the world have been plateauing in 2014 while economic growth was about 3% is another indication that the world may be soon finding a structural way of declining emissions in absolute terms.[1]

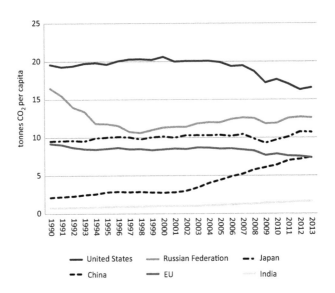

FIGURE 5.3 CO$_2$ emissions *per capita* from fossil-fuel use and cement production
Source: adapted from trends in global CO$_2$ emissions, 2014 Report, PBL, JRC.

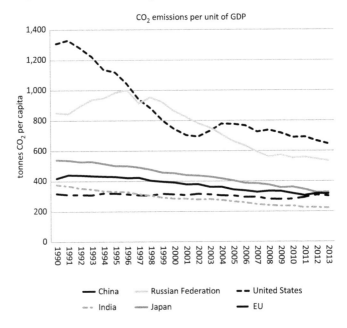

FIGURE 5.4 CO$_2$ emissions *per capita* from fossil-fuel use and cement production per unit of GDP

Sources: trends in global CO$_2$ emissions, 2014 Report, PBL, JRC.

Note: Expressed in GDP unit of: US$1,000 adjusted to the purchasing power parity of 2011, based on IMF, World Bank.

Conclusion: the world has evolved significantly since 1990. The 'firewall' of the UNFCCC, separating the obligations between developed and developing countries, no longer corresponds with the economic realities of the world today.

Setting the foundations for a 2015 Agreement

Recognising the shortcomings of the Copenhagen–Cancun approach and the failure of the Kyoto Protocol to attract more Parties, the UNFCCC agreed in 2011 in Durban to launch negotiations on a new international agreement to be completed by the end of 2015 and to apply from 2020 onwards.

The EU worked closely with progressive allies to agree a 'Durban mandate' for these negotiations that is designed to ensure a result that, unlike the Kyoto Protocol, will be 'applicable to all Parties' and that, unlike the voluntary Copenhagen–Cancun pledges, will be set out in a Protocol or another form of international agreement 'with legal force'.

To help secure this deal, and to reassure developing and emerging countries that industrialised countries will continue to take a leadership role, the EU agreed to enter into a second commitment period under the Kyoto Protocol, from 2012 to 2020. All Parties agreed to make efforts to raise their ambition in that same time period.

Since 2011, the negotiators returned to the challenge of how to set emission reduction targets, applicable to all Parties, which are both ambitious and fair. It became quickly apparent that Parties would be unable to agree an approach that set a global emissions budget for a specific timeframe, or to allocate that budget on the basis of agreed criteria – in the way, for example, the EU negotiates its effort sharing for emissions outside the ETS. It also became clear that Parties were unwilling to agree to a single commitment type, such as the economy-wide emission reduction targets that are part of the Kyoto Protocol.

In this context Parties began to map out the third model of international climate policy – a hybrid approach between the 'top-down' aspects of the Kyoto Protocol and the 'bottom-up' approach of the Copenhagen–Cancun pledges. In Warsaw, in 2013, and in Lima, in 2014, Parties agreed to come forward in the run up to Paris, with 'Intended Nationally Determined Contributions' (INDCs) that will serve as the basis for their commitments in the 2015 Agreement.

Parties agreed that each INDC would represent a contribution towards the UNFCCC objective of limiting dangerous climate change. Each INDC must represent a progression beyond what a Party has committed to already, in the form of domestic policy, an international pledge or target. Each Party must communicate its INDC in a clear and understandable manner, and that explains how that Party considers its commitment will be fair and ambitious, in the light of its national circumstance and of the UNFCCC's ultimate objective to stabilise greenhouse gas concentrations at a safe level. While many countries continue to indicate their reluctance to have their INDCs scrutinised or negotiated through a multilateral process, the international guidance provided by the Warsaw and Lima decisions creates a 'top-down' political expectation of clarity and ambition.

The INDC process has already generated some promising results. In preparation for Paris, the EU Heads of State and Government announced their INDC in October 2014. Shortly thereafter, the US and China made a joint announcement setting out the basic elements of their targets. And there is evidence that many other countries are in the process of preparing their commitment in advance of Paris. The challenge that remains is capturing these commitments, and the commitments of as many countries as possible in a legally binding 2015 Agreement framework that supports their implementation.

Conclusion: a third model of international climate policy seems to be emerging as a hybrid between the 'top-down' aspects of the Kyoto Protocol and the 'bottom-up' approach of the Copenhagen–Cancun pledges.

An EU vision for the 2015 Agreement

Introduction

The EU believes the 2015 Agreement should take the form of a legally binding Protocol to the UNFCCC, as this is the best-understood form of 'legal instrument' the Parties can adopt.[2]

In essence, the Paris Protocol should:

- Secure each Party's INDC in the form of a clear, specific, ambitious and fair legally binding mitigation commitment. Together, these commitments should put the world on track towards achieving the below-2°C objective. These commitments must be consistent with the UNFCCC's principles applied in the light of evolving responsibilities, capabilities and different national circumstances.

- Ensure dynamism by providing for a global review, to be conducted every five years, to strengthen the ambition of these mitigation commitments consistent with the latest science. This review should be guided by a long-term goal to reduce global emissions by at least 60% below 2010 levels by 2050.

- Strengthen transparency and accountability in order to be able to assess whether emission reduction targets and related commitments have been met. A common set of rules and procedures for annual reporting and regular verification and international expert reviews of emission inventories needs to be established.

- Encourage climate-resilient sustainable development by promoting international cooperation and supporting policies that decrease vulnerability and improve countries' capacity to adapt to the impacts of climate change.

- Promote efficient and effective implementation and cooperation by encouraging policies that mobilise substantial, transparent and predictable public and private sector investment in low-emission climate-resilient development.

To join the Agreement, each Party must make a legally binding mitigation commitment. This will give the clearest signal that Parties will commit themselves to provide:

- the strongest expression of a Party's political will to achieve its commitments;
- necessary predictability and certainty for all public and private actors; and
- durability in the context of domestic political changes.

Securing ambitious mitigation commitments

The new Protocol needs to cover, in a comprehensive manner, the bulk of global emissions, to send a strong signal to the public and to the markets that the world is serious about phasing-down greenhouse gas emissions over time. The announcements made by the EU, the US and China, which cover nearly half of global emissions, is a promising first step.

Each Party's INDC should represent a significant progression in the level of mitigation ambition and scope compared to its current pledge. It should demonstrate convergence on low levels of overall emissions and *per capita* emissions and improvement in emission intensity over time.

Countries with the highest responsibilities and capabilities need to have the most ambitious mitigation commitments. Economy-wide absolute targets combined with emission budgets are the most robust commitment type. They have a number of advantages including certainty, transparency, flexibility and, if used widely, reduced risk of carbon leakage. In line with the idea of progression over time, all countries that already have such targets should maintain and increase these against a historic base year or reference period. G20 and other high-income countries that do not have absolute targets under the Protocol from 2020 should commit to doing so by 2025 at the latest. Other emerging economies and middle-income countries are encouraged to do so as early as possible, and not later than 2030.

Parties' commitments must create strong incentives for all actors to further reduce and limit global emissions. The Protocol should require emission reductions in all sectors, including agriculture, forestry and other land uses, international aviation and shipping, and fluorinated gases. The ICAO, IMO and the Montreal Protocol should act to effectively regulate emissions from international aviation and shipping and the production and consumption of fluorinated gases, respectively, by the end of 2016.

Ensuring dynamism through the regular review of targets

The Protocol should set out a process, applicable to all Parties, to regularly review and strengthen mitigation commitments, consistent with the Protocol's long-term goal. If Parties' collective efforts fall short of what is necessary, the process should encourage Parties to raise the level of ambition of existing commitments and formulate sufficiently ambitious commitments in subsequent target periods.

Starting in 2020, the review should be repeated every five years and facilitate transparency, clarity and understanding of mitigation commitments in the light of their contribution to the below-2°C objective. The review should invite Parties to explain progress on their mitigation commitments and why they think their actions have been fair and ambitious.

The process should be informed by science, be evidence based, and be guided by considerations of evolving responsibilities, capabilities and different national circumstances. It should be simple, efficient, and avoid duplication of other processes. The arrangements for the review cycle should be improved over time to stay on track to achieve the below-2°C objective.

The Protocol and accompanying decisions by the Conference of the Parties need to provide for the dynamic mobilisation of climate finance, technology transfer and capacity building for eligible Parties, particularly those with least capabilities. This will include processes to regularly assess and improve the adequacy and effectiveness of the means of implementation mobilised by the UNFCCC. Support for Parties to regularly review and strengthen their approaches to adaptation over time will also need to be ensured in Paris.

Strengthening transparency and accountability

The Protocol must set out the key elements of a common transparency and accountability system, applicable to all Parties. This must include robust rules on monitoring, reporting, verification and accounting, and a process for holding each Party accountable for achieving its commitments. This system will be essential to provide confidence that each Party is implementing its commitments and is on track to meet its target. It will also be crucial to build trust, encourage ambition, and provide predictability and legal certainty. As such, Parties should submit, at the latest by the time of ratification, the most recent set of annual emissions inventories from 2010 covering the period up to 2015.

This system should be fit for the long term. While it must be sufficiently flexible to cater for a diverse range of commitment types, national capabilities and circumstances, this flexibility should not undermine transparency, accountability and ambition. Independent expert review teams should conduct regular reviews. The new Protocol should recognise net transfers between those countries that have decided to link their domestic carbon markets, and this should be taken into account when evaluating compliance.

Finally, the Protocol should establish a body to facilitate implementation and address questions that are raised over compliance with regard to the implementation of any Party's commitments. This body should focus on commitments related to mitigation, including monitoring, reporting, verification and accounting. The body should be expert and non-political, with its mandate to be specified in the Protocol.

Achieving climate resilience through adaptation

While ambitious mitigation action is essential, it will be equally important to encourage individual and collaborative actions to prepare for and adapt to the adverse impacts of climate change. The role of the land-use sector with regard to food security, and other environmental, social and economic benefits is key to this work. The EU's strategy on adaptation, complementing Member States' strategies, aims to develop a more climate-resilient Europe. Ecosystem-based adaptation can reduce flood risk and soil erosion as well as improve water and air quality.

In the context of achieving climate-resilient sustainable development of all Parties, the Protocol should reinforce the commitments of all Parties to continue to formulate, plan and implement measures to facilitate adaptation and to report on these through their national communications. The Protocol should continue to facilitate assistance to those regions and countries that are particularly vulnerable to the adverse effects of climate change, including the provision of financial and technical support and capacity-building.

In this way the Protocol will provide further visibility for adaptation action and support, and strengthen the monitoring and reporting provisions under the UNFCCC. It will also enable greater understanding of the effectiveness of measures carried out to facilitate adequate adaptation, drawing on national reports and other relevant information in order to inform further enhanced action to be undertaken by Parties.

Mobilising public and private climate finance

The transformation into low-emission climate-resilient economies will only be achieved through large-scale shifts in investment patterns. The Protocol should promote investments in low-emission climate-resilient programmes and policies. All countries should commit to take steps to improve their enabling of environments for attracting climate-friendly investments. Countries in a position to do so should mobilise financial support for eligible Parties to the Protocol. The base of financial support needs to be broadened over time as capabilities of Parties change. Clarity should also be provided by all Parties on the climate impact of financial flows that do not fall within the remit of climate finance.

Public sector climate finance will continue to play an important role in mobilising resources after 2020. The Protocol should also recognise the importance of the private sector as a key source to scaling up climate finance. The Protocol should provide assurances to the poorest countries and those most vulnerable to climate change that they will continue to receive priority support.

The Protocol should promote the formulation and implementation of strong enabling environments for the transformation to low-emission climate-resilient economies including:

- ambitious national climate policies;
- effective governance, including investment frameworks, price incentives and financing instruments favouring low-emission and climate-resilient investments; and
- providing information on how to address climate change.

Carbon pricing and the investment policies of public development banks will play a central role in this. Mainstreaming climate considerations into all policies, development strategies and investments is essential to make use of the synergies between development, mitigation and adaptation financing.

Conclusion: the core of the 2015 Agreement will basically consist of each Party's Intended Nationally Determined Contributions; a process on how to review and adopt new contributions in the future; and arrangements related to transparency and accountability. Climate finance will be important to facilitate the transformation towards a low-carbon economy.

Conclusions

The UNFCCC process has been too slow in delivering the outcomes and impacts necessary to put the world on a path towards a stable climate system. But two decades of trying has laid a solid foundation for the essential next step in the formulation of international climate policy – the preparation of ambitious domestic legislation and regulation by the world's largest economies, and the willingness of these countries to hold themselves regularly accountable for the implementation of these policies.

Early indications are that this process of policy formulation, stimulated by consistent demands that all countries demonstrate how they are contributing to this collective challenge, is indeed taking place in all major economies. This seems in part to have resulted from a much deeper and widely shared understanding of climate science, and of how most countries will suffer from the impacts of climate change. Governments, businesses and civil society across countries in diverse circumstances are sharing an appreciation of the co-benefits – from improvements in local air quality, to greater energy independence – that can be generated by more ambitious climate policy. And there seems to be a growing awareness that first-movers on low-carbon policies and technologies are likely to emerge more competitive in tomorrow's markets.

Twenty years of experimentation in policymaking and institution-building under the UNFCCC has also built a better appreciation of what functions the next generation of the international climate regime can and should perform. As countries adopt more ambitious climate policies they will be increasingly concerned that their trading partners follow suit. Only a successive strengthening of national and regional policies will deliver the emission reductions required by science. These policies will undoubtedly have some trade effects, at least in the short term. The UNFCCC, however, must generate comparable policy efforts by all countries with significant emissions if trade tensions are to be avoided in the future.

It is, therefore, also of capital importance that an international climate regime provides a high level of transparency, comparability and accountability so as to reassure economic competitors across multiple sectors that they are competing on a level playing field. Similarly, as more countries opt to create and possibly link markets in carbon allowances, they will appreciate some basic rules being agreed in an international climate regime to promote fungibility and liquidity as well as help prevent fraud and double-counting.

Finally, the future international climate regime will need to continue to provide a forum that regularly brings together evolving climate science with political leadership at the highest possible level. The third way that is now on the table for Paris may also serve as a good example for addressing future global challenges in a multilateral context. What seems to be required is excellent science, political leadership as well as a solid reassurance that all countries contribute to the solution of the problem in a fair and balanced manner, basically building further on their domestically formulated policies.

> Conclusion: the essential next step to be taken after a successful 2015 Agreement in Paris would be for the world's largest economies to develop domestic policies consistent with their commitments, and for them to be prepared to be held regularly accountable for the effective implementation of these policies.

Notes

1 See IEA: www.iea.org/newsroomandevents/news/2015/march/global-energy-related-emissions-of-carbon-dioxide-stalled-in-2014.html

2 European Commission (2015) 'The Paris Protocol - A blueprint for tackling global climate change beyond 2020'. COM(2015) 81 final/2 and its Annex 1 of 4.3.2015, and the accompanying Commission Staff Working Document SWD(2015) 17 final of 25.2.2015: http://ec.europa.eu/clima/policies/international/paris_protocol/docs/com_2015_81_en.pdf and Annex 1 to the above: http://ec.europa.eu/clima/policies/international/paris_protocol/docs/com_2015_81_annex_en.pdf and Accompanying Staff Working Document: http://ec.europa.eu/clima/policies/international/paris_protocol/docs/swd_2015_17_en.pdf

6

OUTLOOK

Jos Delbeke and Peter Vis

Policymaking backdrop

Climate policy in the EU started in the 1990s with its active involvement in the relevant international processes, such as the Intergovernmental Panel on Climate Change (IPCC) and the United Nations Framework Convention on Climate Change (UNFCCC).

Much effort was invested by the IPCC in establishing a consensus among almost all climate scientists in the world on what we know, and do not know, about climate change. With the finalisation of the Fifth Assessment Report in 2014, a further and substantial piece of convincing evidence has been provided. Climate change is happening in a way that is unprecedented over decades, centuries and millennia. What had been proved as well is that this is happening as a result of human influences, in particular since the Industrial Revolution of the eighteenth century. Since then, the world's use of fossil fuels – the major contributor to climate change – has kept increasing to today's levels. Scientists tell us that, if we want to avoid dangerous impacts of climate change, we should not allow the average global temperature to rise beyond 2°C compared to pre-industrial levels. This implies that the world as a whole should be peaking its emissions by no later than 2020, and then halve its emissions by 2050.

The other major piece of international governance in which the EU has invested considerable effort is the UNFCCC process. The Framework Convention on Climate Change was adopted in 1992 at the UN Summit on

Sustainable Development in Rio de Janeiro. The first major operational decisions were made through the agreement of the Kyoto Protocol in 1997. That Protocol, reflecting the Annexes to the Convention, divided the obligations of Parties between quantitative emission limitation or reduction commitments for developed countries, on the one hand, and the rest of the world on the other, without binding quantitative commitments. What seemed logical in the 1990s, however, has become increasingly less so as many of these developing countries transformed into emerging economies with higher annual emissions than many developed countries. The economic and industrial rise of China since the year 2000 is one of the most striking elements in this respect.

This sharp division between developed and developing nations undermined the effectiveness of the Kyoto Protocol, and remains the Achilles heel of the multilateral approach to climate change. The US did not ratify the Kyoto Protocol as a result, Canada shunned its obligations, and Australia and Japan are unwilling to take on a second commitment through to 2020. Only the EU, together with Norway, Iceland and Switzerland, delivered on their obligations and assumed new ones until 2020. However, climate change cannot be halted if only some 12% of global emissions are covered by emission reduction commitments. The challenge for the upcoming Paris Climate Change Conference in December of 2015 is to find a new way of involving all countries in undertaking action, albeit in a differentiated manner, consistent with what science tells us is necessary.

Fairness and cost-effectiveness

The EU has useful experience when it comes to differentiation of efforts to reduce greenhouse gas emissions. The EU is seen as a homogeneous group of developed countries although in fact there is considerable diversity between them. A considerable number of its Member States have wealth *per capita* similar to many developing countries, or emerging economies. When the EU prepared domestic policies to deliver on its Kyoto Protocol obligations, sufficient differentiation between the efforts being asked of each Member State was a condition for agreement. The EU therefore distributed its efforts and compliance costs in line with the relative wealth of its Member States by differentiating these according to their GDP *per capita*.

For the EU not only fairness mattered but also the overall cost-effectiveness of its policies, as climate policy measures show very different cost patterns. If low-cost options are implemented first, then more reductions can be realised. And choosing highest-cost options would ultimately limit ambition by exhausting the willingness to pay of governments and consumers. This willingness to pay was further tested by the fact that many of the EU's trading partners had no binding international reductions obligations. Yet these domestic climate policies were being developed at a moment when the EU was experiencing rapid globalisation in the 1990s and 2000s. So, cost considerations have always been of capital importance in delivering the significant emission reductions that the EU has committed to at the international level.

Two major lines of action were taken to ensure fairness and cost-efficiency. The first is that policies at EU level were pursued in areas where it made sense in the context of the internal market to facilitate economies of scale and market-driven efficiencies, thereby keeping costs as low as possible. The EU ETS, covering all major industrial installations in power generation and manufacturing, established a unified market for emission reductions. The EU ETS treated all participating companies in exactly the same manner, and reaped low-cost options first across the EU. At the same time important energy-relevant products, such as cars, transport fuels and energy-consuming appliances, were subject to harmonised regulations, as the only way to avoid trade distortions and barriers inside the EU's internal market. Also some specific regulations were developed, such as for fluorinated gases, as a limited number of key players were mainly large companies operating in the EU market.

The other major line of action concerned the millions of individual consumers in very diverse economic and social circumstances. For these emissions, from housing, transport, and agriculture, the obligations of Member States were differentiated according to their relative wealth, expressed by GDP *per capita*. But to keep costs low and acceptable, much attention was given to flexibility provisions allowed to the Member States. This flexibility was therefore designed into the Effort Sharing Decision, and into the legislation related to renewable energy or energy efficiency. It is to be expected that, as 2020 approaches, more effort will be made by Member States to use these flexibilities in order to keep costs down.

This combination of fairness and cost-efficiency has already delivered significant emission reductions. A significant decoupling of emissions from economic growth has been sustained since 1990: economic growth has increased by 45% to 2013 while emissions have decreased by 19%. The key to this was technological developments in all sectors, but even more important was to actually deploy these technological developments in everyday life. Through its regulations, the EU offered a huge market for these technologies and became a champion in low-carbon and highly energy-efficient equipment, products and services, and in doing so created millions of new high-quality jobs. At the same time it has prepared itself for deeper emission reductions in the future through a systematic encouragement of research and innovation in this area, in particular through the EU's €80 billion 'Horizon 2020' Research and Development programme, the Energy Union framework, and through a remarkable increase in patents for low-carbon technologies.[1]

EU record of achievement

This book has explained how the EU learned and established its policies. After making a start, and, in the light of experience, refinements were introduced, and this will undoubtedly continue in the future. Perhaps a relatively 'hidden' part of its experience is the understanding of how important a solid monitoring and accounting system of its emissions is. Out of its obligations based on Articles 5, 7 and 8 of the Kyoto Protocol, the EU has put in place the mechanisms it needs to accurately track, year on year, its emissions without there being arguments among practitioners and scientists. Such data have offered a transparent basis for the further refinement of measures or for concentration on areas that need to be brought to the attention of the policymakers, such as forestry and land-use emissions.

For the Paris Agreement that is in preparation, or for further action in the context of the ICAO and IMO on aviation and maritime sectors respectively, three major lessons can be drawn from the EU's experience. The first is that the monitoring, reporting and verification of emissions (MRV) are of capital importance. Decisions on this must complement the submissions by Parties of their Intended Nationally Determined Contributions. Transparent and comparable data on emissions should be the 'cement' among Parties that ensures the building of trust, and which inspires the development of future policies. The second lesson is that sufficient differentiation of policies and ambition levels between Parties can ensure a fair distribution of mitigation effort. The richer you are, the more you should be ready to contribute to the solutions, and this must go beyond the simplistic divide between developed and developing countries that is now largely out of date. The third lesson is about cost-effectiveness: maintaining public support for action makes the prioritisation of low-cost policies essential, both because it allows for more action, but also because it limits any potential trade disputes between Parties.

It is sometimes said that the EU's record of achievement in reducing its emissions of greenhouse gas is flattered by the methodology used, which is to count the direct emissions related to production rather than the indirect emissions of imported goods consumed. First, that criticism is above all criticism of the partial coverage of quantitative climate commitments under the Kyoto Protocol, which are limited to industrialised countries. The Paris Agreement should correct that. Second, the direct emissions approach, used by the IPCC and the UNFCCC has been agreed internationally and is more feasible to implement from a monitoring, reporting and verification perspective. Third, an indirect emissions, or consumption-based, approach, as advocated by some, would logically require that emissions of third countries be included within the scope of the domestic climate policies of the country of consumption, which would pose such challenges of implementation and enforcement as to be unfeasible. Developing countries are not in favour of such an approach, which would impose carbon constraints on their factories and production without taking account of different levels of development between countries (as reflected by indicators such as greenhouse gas emissions *per capita* or GDP *per capita*). Finally, developing countries also fear that an indirect emissions, or consumption-based, approach could also lead to the imposition of border tax adjustments. That could trigger trade disputes that are better avoided through a wide participation of all countries in a multilateral agreement.

What lessons does the EU draw from its experience to date? The EU has realised that climate policies need to be integrated into its 'normal' economic policies, in particular to ensure maximum coherence between climate and energy policy. EU leaders underlined this need for coherence through their decisions at the European Councils of October 2014, on the Climate and Energy framework for 2030, and on the establishment of a European Energy Union, in March 2015[2]. They underlined that the five dimensions of an Energy Union are deeply interrelated: (1) energy security, solidarity and trust; (2) a fully integrated European energy market; (3) energy efficiency contributing to moderation of demand; (4) decarbonising the economy; and (5) research, innovation and competitiveness.

The preparation of further policies will assess increasingly the relation between environmental ambition, energy prices and competitiveness. Furthermore, by working in 'packages' of measures developed, proposed and adopted simultaneously, the integration of political decision-making is enhanced. This process is likely to put increasing emphasis on flexibilities that would enable greater cost-effectiveness of policies. Evidence of such flexibilities extends beyond the more obvious use of market-based instruments, such as emissions trading, but also includes the flexibilities of the regulation on the CO_2 performance of passenger cars, the cooperation between Member States on renewable energy, and, more recently, the choice by the European Council to impose neither Member State-specific renewable energy targets nor energy-efficiency targets for 2030.

Another major change in policymaking, as mentioned in Chapter 4, is the mainstreaming of climate action and energy objectives into the EU's budget. The EU has resolved that at least 20% of its budget for the years 2014 to 2020 would be spent in direct or indirect relation to climate change. This amounts to some €180 billion, in the major policy domains such as regional development, agriculture and research and development. Structural and Cohesion funds, for example, can assist lower-income Member States with a high potential for energy-efficiency improvements to invest in buildings renovation, refurbishment of district heating systems, and the replacement or upgrading of ageing infrastructure. In 2014, climate-related expenditure of the EU budget amounted to 15.5%, and determination exists to keep increasing this figure.

Until now, the EU's record of achievement and 'climate leadership' has been with regard to its emissions performance, judged against the internationally agreed yardstick. Leadership has also been provided, as described in this book, as a laboratory of 'learning-by-doing' which has enabled considerable experience to be gained. It is hoped that this could be of benefit to all countries, and improve the effectiveness of climate policies over time.

> Conclusion: the European institutions are investing much effort to improve the preparation of the EU's climate policies through the systematic assessment of costs, benefits and distributive effects. The EU has acquired considerable expertise in differentiating effort between diverse EU Member States so as to ensure fairness. Cost-effectiveness considerations and flexibilities in implementation are key. This is being done within the internationally agreed accounting framework of the direct emissions approach.

Notes

1   EU companies have a share of 40% of all patents for renewable technologies, compared to a 32% EU share in overall global patents (source: European Commission COM(2015) 80 final of 25.2.2015).
2   European Council conclusions of 19-20 March 2015, document EUCO 11/15 dated 20 March 2015: www.consilium.europa.eu/en/press/press-releases/2015/03/20-conclusions-european-council

INDEX

For Product Safety Concerns and Information please contact our EU representative GPSR@taylorandfrancis.com
Taylor & Francis Verlag GmbH, Kaufingerstraße 24, 80331 München, Germany